Conversations of the Heart

Conversations
of the *Heart*

Woodie W. White

Abingdon Press

Nashville

CONVERSATIONS OF THE HEART

Copyright © 1991 by Woodie W. White

This book is printed on acid-free paper.

Library of Congress Cataloging-in-Publication Data

White, Woodie W., 1935-
    Conversations of the Heart / Woodie W. White.
      p.   cm.
    ISBN 0-687-09637-5 (alk. paper)
    1. Spiritual life—Methodist authors. I. Title.
BV4501.2.W467   1991
248.4'87—dc20   90-48507
                                                 CIP

Scripture noted NRSV is from the New Revised Standard Version Bible, copyright © 1989, by the Division of Christian Education of the National Council of the Churches of Christ in the United States of America. Used by permission.

Scripture noted Phillips is from The New Testament in Modern English, copyright © J. B. Phillips 1958, 1960, 1972. Used by permission.

MANUFACTURED IN THE UNITED STATES OF AMERICA

To
Captolia Dent Newbern,
who had more faith in me
than I had in myself

Contents

Contents

Conversations
of the Heart

Editor's Note

Born and raised in New York City, Woodie W. White, after graduating from Paine College in Georgia and Boston University School of Theology, spent his life as a cleric in Detroit, Baltimore, and Washington, D.C. He came to the Illinois prairie in 1984 after being elected a bishop of The United Methodist Church at Duluth, Minnesota. His Episcopal Area of the denomination includes Central and Southern Illinois.

As editor of the Central Illinois Conference edition of *The United Methodist Reporter*, I invited the new bishop to write a column for clergy and church members. He responded with weekly contributions no matter what his schedule, responsibilities, or travel commitments. His faithfulness demonstrated his desire to communicate with the "precious people of God."

Out of this commitment *Conversations of the Heart* and a companion volume, *Confessions of a Prairie Pilgrim* (Abingdon Press, 1988), were born. As Bishop White expresses his love for and expectations of Christians, he enters into conversations with us straight from the heart that pry and pain, challenge and comfort, as he shares his concerns and consolations. His invitation is compelling to enter into heart-talk with him as seekers of truth and faith through Jesus the Christ.

Bettie Wilson Story
Editor

Introduction

As a boy I used to talk to myself. Often the conversations were in whispered tones, but I distinctly recall hearing my words. The conversations were sometimes games I played alone. At times they were imaginary with a hero or fictitious character, or with the neighborhood bully, but seldom repeated in his presence.

As I grew older the nature and character of these conversations changed. At some point I learned that talking to oneself was unacceptable, indeed questionable, behavior. I often wonder why these special conversations continued. Was it out of loneliness or some unmet need?

Occasionally a parent or other member of the family would hear and chastise or question me. But mostly my conversations went undetected and uninterrupted. They ceased to be audible and became mind and spirit conversations. The words, rarely spoken, were nonetheless distinct and clear.

As I reflect now in adulthood I am aware of the significant influence words have had in my maturation and my faith development. To be able to think, to reflect, and to speak thoughts, ideas, and feelings are gifts of the human spirit.

Soon one learns, however, that conversation must be guarded and moderated. One's context dictates what is said and how. The innocence of youth, when one speaks the naked truth, is quickly corrected. Thus we learn to dress truth and words, sometimes so carefully as to camouflage both. Or we learn what "truth" is expected or accepted, and we shape and choose our words so that our conversation meets the test of acceptability.

Clever persons learn a kind of double-speak—saying what they desire in such a manner that the hearer does not understand what is really being said but hears what he or she wants to hear. There is a private consolation in knowing that one has spoken one's mind without having paid the price of uttering truth.

Silent conversation or self-conversation avoids these traps and challenges, but it can become monologue instead of dialogue, the prerequisite of conversation.

Sir William Melmoth, an eighteenth-century English author, once said, "Conversation opens our views, and gives our faculties a more vigorous play; it puts us upon turning our notions on every side, and holds them up to a light that discovers these latest flaws which would probably have lain concealed in the gloom of unagitated abstraction."

In a curious way my silent conversations always seem dialogical. Present is the other to whom I am either speaking or responding: friend, foe, God. Often the conversations are joyous, causing the heart to sing or laugh or dance; too often their pain causes sadness and weeping. Expressed ideas, hurts, and frustrations find a listener or more often than not an inquisitor, questioning, prying, forcing me deeper. Sometimes the conversations involve the Comforter, who soothes the hurts, heals the scarred places, and turns despair to hope.

The little boy has grown into the man who still has those daily and nightly conversations, those moments when the heart opens and is touched by another or by some thought or deed or when the heart must speak first to God and sometimes only to God.

At times the conversations in this volume will be with God, and you will be a bystander. Sometimes they will be with that neighborhood bully I knew as a child who has simply grown up, moved elsewhere, and taken on different identities.

Occasionally the conversations are with the writer, and it will be obvious that he is oblivious to the reader. There will be moments when I am right and others when I am wrong. These are the ways of the heart. It will be honest, sometimes painfully and embarrassingly so.

What you will find in these pages is not intended to be pronouncements and commands to be followed or to which you are expected to subscribe. Sometimes it may appear so. But rather I would like to think you will be listening to conversations—conversations of the heart.

Woodie W. White
Springfield, Illinois

Face to Face with God

Some spiritual experiences are so high and yet so deep that words are inadequate and would only trivialize what the soul and heart have experienced. Perhaps that is what happened to Mary at the birth of the Christ Child. Words would have been insufficient, so Luke records that she "kept all these things, and pondered them in her heart."

Then face to face

The landscape on the day following the first major snowfall resembled a painted portrait: a brilliant blue sky and the sun glistening off freshly fallen snow that was whiter than white. It was a day to be outdoors. Kim suggested that I get out my cross-country skis, which have seen little use the past few years. My body said no, and I agreed, so I ventured to the nearby park for a walk.

Once in the park my spirits continued high and exuberant. Children and adults on sleds had congregated at a popular hill for sledding. I kind of envied a number of people on cross-country skis, except those who obviously were not having fun. Older and younger couples were holding hands as they trudged through the soft snow. It was a Norman Rockwell scene.

Suddenly, in the midst of all this happiness, sadness came upon me. Infuriated that such serenity was interrupted by unpleasant thoughts, I attempted to clear my mind, erase whatever was causing the change in mood. Then I noticed the familiar face of a person walking beside me. Was this a member of one of our congregations, a neighbor, even a pastor? My mind raced to recall as I said, "Good morning."

The response came in a friendly tone, "Good morning. What a beautiful day!"

I had planned to say no more. Subtly I increased my pace so as not to be alongside the stranger. My new friend did likewise and then asked the question I dreaded.

"Do you remember me?"

I tried my best to put the familiar face in a place but for the life of me could not. "I'm sorry," I responded. "I know you, but I just can't put the face and name together."

"Well, I confess I didn't think you would recognize me. At least I hoped you wouldn't!"

I was puzzled by this response, but I looked more closely for some clue that would give me a name, a place.

"Now I know," I blurted out. "You're God, aren't you?"

God didn't acknowledge my response, but I knew it was God.

Continuing as though I had not spoken, God said, "I like to keep people off guard just a bit. Too many have already categorically described me by race, gender, class, nationality, even political party."

Now I realized the source of my change of mood from happiness to sadness and had to get it off my chest.

"May I be candid with you, God?"

"Of course. You've never hesitated in the past."

"Well, I'm upset! Angry, sad, confused. Feeling somewhat frustrated and helpless."

The only response was a knowing and sympathetic glance. So I continued.

"There's just too much violence and suffering in the world. Almost everywhere you look, there's war and enmity. Atrocities, committed by neighbor against neighbor, nation against nation, tribe against tribe, seem unending."

I continued, wanting to get it all out of my system, "The bombing of the Pan Am jet killed all aboard as well as residents in Lockerbie.

"But, God, equally troubling is the recent earthquake that took the lives of thousands and devastated an entire community. And the hurricanes. These are sometimes called acts of God." I wanted God to feel some sense of responsibility.

I looked for some change of expression, perhaps annoyance or anger, but what I saw was sadness.

"It just doesn't make sense, God! It's not fair. Is there no end to it? The suffering, violence, and tragedy seem to escalate. Why God? Why?"

I had gotten it all out but felt no sense of relief as I expected. Now I felt guilty. I sounded like one who lacked faith or trust. I was half sorry I had said all these things. Perhaps I could have said them a little more diplomatically or at least respectfully.

Then God said, "I understand. When you get home from your walk read I Corinthians 13:12."

God then put an arm around my shoulder, and we walked through the snow in silence.

Ponderings of the heart

I heard the sermon preached thirty-five years ago, and I remember the text to this day. It is interesting what the mind selects for recall. Why I remember that particular text is still a mystery.

It was the Sunday before Christmas, and the congregation was excited. The four choirs that sang each Sunday were well rehearsed for the special Christmas music, and the sanctuary was decorated with the traditional greens of Christmas. Clearly this was a special day.

We awaited the sermon with great expectation. Our pastor was a powerful and dramatic pulpiteer and one of the greatest manuscript preachers I have ever heard. While I don't recall his sermon topic that day, his text has remained with me all these years: "But Mary kept all these things, and pondered them in her heart" (Luke 2:19). There are times for heart-pondering.

Some years ago a saying in vogue was, "Let it all hang out!" In that age of free expression, persons were encouraged to say what was on their minds and in their hearts. In some circles the idea was carried to actions as well—not only say what you will but do what you will.

Soon this spirit of free expression was a part of many groups both in and outside of the church. Persons were encouraged to be brutally candid, and many were. For some individuals great good resulted; others still carry the scars of that time of free, uninhibited expression and action.

At times expressions of the soul's yearnings are helpful and needful. Sometimes release comes only when one is able to articulate to another what is on the mind and in the heart. Yet other moments are so precious that they are times of heart-pondering.

Every emotion need not be expressed even to those close and dear. Some may be so utterly personal that to share them with another would violate their inherent integrity. They require heart care—inward and personal reflection and pondering.

Some spiritual experiences are so high and yet so deep that words are inadequate and would only trivialize what the soul and heart have experienced. Perhaps that is what happened to Mary at the birth of the Christ Child. Words would have been insufficient, so Luke records that she "kept all these things, and pondered them in her heart."

Sometimes experiences of love are that way. While love must always find expression, not every expression of love can be expressed. It is for heart-pondering. No word or act could possibly convey the full measure of feeling and emotion.

Likewise, some condition, deed, or thought may cause such pain that sharing it is too heavy a burden for others to bear. Letting it all hang out might be a great disservice to those who are most loved and valued. They are better left to heart-pondering and God-sharing.

So life's drama continues, giving each of us an array of experiences and carrying us on emotional and spiritual journeys never imagined. Surprises along the way are as certain as are joys, tears, and disappointments. Memories help us recall what we want to remember and sometimes what we desperately want to forget. But to speak them is not always essential or even judicious.

Some of the highest and lowest moments in life are reserved. They should be marked, "For God only," and then carefully encased and kept to ponder in your heart.

When tempted to defend Christ . . . resist!

I watched with considerable detachment and only slight interest a great deal of furor over a film entitled *The Last Temptation of Christ.* I read the book when it was published in the 1950s, and it is still on my library shelf. I had forgotten all about it. But I used some passages from it to introduce a Lenten sermon.

I don't intend to see the film. Neither will I picket a theater where it is shown, or recommend that others not see it.

What disappointed me most as I listened to the debate over the movie is how un-Christly some are in their zeal to defend the person and divinity of Jesus Christ. Frankly, I think Jesus does not need defenders. He needs witnesses.

Strange things have happened in the history of the church when its adherents have taken the position of defenders of the faith. Usually the defenders demanded unreasonable conformity and a narrow orthodoxy. Soon intolerance followed. Wars have been fought in the name of defending the faith.

We believe that Jesus, the center of our faith, is to be praised, honored, and, more important, followed. That is why we who choose to follow him are called Christian disciples: It is our responsibility, and no one else's, in my judgment, to praise and honor him. We praise, adore, worship, and follow him. I don't require or expect governments, schools, or mass media to assume the responsibility of the church and disciples.

We are to be witnesses, not defenders! We witness to the lordship of Christ and to his divinity. We do not try to out-shout those who believe otherwise.

Jesus will not be more or less divine by what or how he is portrayed by Hollywood. A long time ago a mob and a government tried to destroy him, and they failed. I doubt that a two-hour movie will succeed today. More likely, however, those who say they are his disciples will attract others to him or detract them from him.

When we try to defend Jesus, our behavior and attitudes lose their moral and ethical integrity when they display the very antithesis of who he is and what he proclaimed.

Distorted faces in rage and hatred defending the Lord of love are the height of incongruity. Threatening those who choose to exercise their constitutional rights to view a movie, however distasteful to faithful Christians, does not gain converts but is more likely to repulse them.

Jesus is not like a nation that requires our defense. He is

altogether holy, sovereign, and immortal. It is the defending of Jesus in the faith that has resulted in such religious intolerance, disunity, and discord within the body of Christ—the church. I suppose we have failed in reaching more men and women for Christ because we have failed to witness to this blessed reality.

God could have chosen another way to be revealed to the world. God has the power to make believers, to give them no choice, to force the human family to say yes. But that was not God's way. God chose Jesus and said that he is the way. Remarkably God has trusted us to get the message out, spreading it abroad with our witness—not our defense.

It is unnecessary for Jesus to be surrounded by Christians and defended from the world or those who would defame his name. He came to save the world. Christians don't need to protect Jesus from "nasty" things that people might say about him, but rather it was his instruction that we overcome evil with good, not with corresponding evil.

We cannot witness to Christ in un-Christly ways. One can be firm but respectful, disagree without being disagreeable. If the Christ proclaimed has not changed us, it is unlikely that others will believe he can change them. To that extent, the medium is the message!

We need fewer defenders of the faith and more witnesses to the saving power of Jesus Christ.

In God talk, who listens?

I was startled by the ring of the doorbell at 3:00 A.M.! I jumped from the bed into my robe and slippers and nervously walked to the door. Surely it must be an emergency; otherwise, no one would visit at this hour.

"Who's there?" I asked before opening the door.

"It's God!"

I didn't recognize the voice. It didn't sound like God. In fact, the person had a strange accent.

I opened the door, and, sure enough, it was God. I invited God in. We sat at the kitchen table. I offered to make coffee, even though I had given it up for Lent. God politely declined—didn't have much time, God said, just needed to talk with me.

I must really be in trouble, I thought, but I maintained at least outward composure. "Well, what do you want to talk about, God?" I asked nervously.

"I thought you might give me some insight into this God talk debate."

"Me?" Recognizing immediately that was grammatically incorrect, I stammered, "I mean, I? Why, you're God!"

God replied, "And you're the bishop!"

"What exactly do you want to know, God? I haven't been that involved in the debate. With two annual conferences to administer, being a parent to four daughters and trying to keep up with all the social and political upheaval, I just haven't had much time to get very involved in the discussions. Besides, I haven't even done my taxes yet! So I don't think I'll be much help. But you're God, and you know everything!"

"Yes," replied God, "but you humans really have me baffled. Every time I think I understand you, you come up with something new. First you argued whether I was one or many, in heaven or on earth. Then you argued whether I was dead or alive, black or white. Now I understand there is great clamor about my gender—if I am he or she or it."

"That's very important for some people," I admitted. "Some get very upset if you are addressed as Father; others get upset if you are not. Others don't like neutering you or simply describing you in adjectives. It's a sensitive issue."

"I know," said God. "That's why I'm so concerned. So many good people seem to be acting in uncharitable ways over this thing. Well, Woodie—may I call you Woodie?"

"Yes."

"You're the bishop. Tell me what you think."

"About what?"

"About this God language," replied God.

"God, I think both sides are taking it a bit far. In fact, I don't think it's really about you anymore."

"What do you mean, not about me? I thought it was all about me."

I continued hesitantly, not wanting to offend God or my brothers and sisters. "God, I think for many it's more about posturing and positioning. It's about culture and egos, winning and losing. It's about being in and out. It's about our little theologies trying to contain a reality beyond any theology. It's even becoming political. Frankly, God, I think that for some you long ago faded into the background of this debate."

"Why do you say that, Woodie?"

"Well, the Bible says that God is love. I kind of measure everything from that premise. When you are the center of life, then love abounds. I don't see or feel much love in many of those engaged in this debate. In fact, what I'm seeing increasingly is intimidation, threats, a kind of self-righteousness, and I'm afraid a big dose of spiritual and theological immaturity."

"It does disturb me," said God, "to know that I am the cause of so much trouble. I thought I would bring the human family together, not be the reason for further division."

"Just remember, God, that I said it's not really about you but about us."

"Thanks for your time, Bishop, I mean Woodie, and I'm sorry to have come at this hour, but somebody told me you probably wouldn't be asleep anyway."

"But, God, won't you stay the night? We've got an extra bed this year with our daughter away at college."

"No, I've got another visit to make."

"At this hour?"

"Yes," said God. "I'm going to see the Southern Baptist minister across town. There's a debate going on with them, you know, as to whether I'm three or one, and I thought that was settled long ago!"

I bid God good night and quietly returned to bed. My wife, Kim, asked drowsily, "Who was at the door?"

"God," I responded reluctantly.

"Sure," she said and went back to sleep.

But I couldn't sleep because it dawned on me that I forgot to ask if God is he, she, or it, and for the life of me I couldn't recall!

Questions about Jesus

What would Jesus do? This probing question has been raised by authors, an assortment of religious leaders, and others. It has been the title of sermons and the subject of debates and seminars.

Usually the focus has been to direct or influence decisions and behavior more than to ponder the ethical decisions of Jesus. The question, however, is not totally devoid of genuine wonder at how Jesus would respond to a multiplicity of ethical decisions not enumerated in Scripture but faced by today's Christian. It is not a frivolous question.

Many are helped when facing complex questions and dilemmas by asking, "What would Jesus do?" While I have more than once introduced the question in my decision making, other, more frequent, questions about Jesus have caused me great wonder.

From time to time I wondered, "What would Jesus be?" It may not have the same theological impact of "What would Jesus do?" but I find it intriguing.

As a thirty-three-year-old young adult, what would Jesus be today? I wonder. Would he be an American, a Russian, or an Israeli? If an American, would he be an easterner, westerner, midwesterner, or southerner?

Would he be a yuppie, a farmer, or perhaps a teacher? Would Jesus again be a carpenter? I wonder if he would belong to the union.

I wonder if the twentieth-century Jesus would be a Democrat, a Republican, or an Independent.

Assuming he would be a Christian, would he be Roman Catholic, Eastern Orthodox, or Protestant?

And I wonder, would Jesus be United Methodist, Baptist, Episcopalian, Presbyterian?

Would Jesus be fundamentalist, liberal, or conservative? Is it possible he would be charismatic?

So what would Jesus be? Would he be *hawk* or *dove*, a *nuke* or *anti-nuke*?

Would he be an Elk, a Moose, or an Odd-Fellow? Indeed, would he be an odd fellow?

Would Jesus be a layperson, a cleric, or a diaconal minister? Would he be a bishop, a district superintendent, or a local pastor? Or I wonder if he would be an "Appointment Beyond the Local Church"?

Would Jesus be at First Church or Last Church? In a rural or city church—or no church?

Would Jesus be pro-choice, pro-busing, or pro-gun control? I wonder, would Jesus be an environmentalist?

Would Jesus be famous or just another obscure member of the human family? Would he be popular? Would he be persecuted?

As I struggle in this complex world nearing the end of the twentieth century, I do seek to be like Jesus. But I wonder how Jesus would fare if he had to be like me, that is, live in our world with its complex ethical dilemmas, myriad religious expressions and choices, and secularism and humanism every bit as profound as in Jesus' day. I wonder.

So it is not an unreasonable question for me to wonder not only what would Jesus do but what would Jesus be. Even as I wonder, I wonder if he would be amused.

Where in the world is God?

Where does God reside? It is not a new question. Neither is the phenomenon of locating God. The ancients believed that God had to be carried from place to place. Others suggested that God was permanently located, usually in their locale.

Contemporaries seem to have a way of knowing precisely where God is. On a recent visit to a beautiful location in the United States, I discovered the residents had a saying that went something like this: "I don't know where God lives, but when God wants to play, God comes here!"

Many times I've heard said in other places, more with arrogance than pride, "This is God's country," suggesting that God would not or could not inhabit other, less desirable locales.

By their actions, if not words, others suggest that God resides in the United States. One heroine in a novel I read questioned if God lived in the poor section of town.

I suppose God listens with wonderment, amusement, and perhaps a twinge of sadness as we conjecture about God's residence. Some peoples have been known to go to war about it.

Occasionally I think that many persons are not altogether jesting when they suggest that God could not live in a place such as New York. Perhaps God's location could be Dallas, St. Louis, or Nashville. Many are certain that it is Nashville! Someone else told me that God wouldn't visit the city, much less live there. Even a visit after certain hours would be out of the question. I suspect some yankees think that God would not live in the South and some southerners are certain God could not live in the North.

God's *place* is often attributed to the activity of people themselves. That is, when people do "God things," they assume God is present. The more God things performed, the more evident is God's presence. People often think or act in a way that suggests God must be summoned to their place. I suppose they surmise that God is at least in earshot, so they call God from that nearby location.

They have been known to debate how God should be summoned. I wonder if distance dictated the mode: Some have suggested that God could be summoned only by an organ, others have insisted by drum, while others have said it must be by piano. Some would claim that God is partial to the guitar. Others say God responds only to a chant, shout, or silence. I imagine some think of God as playing a kind of cosmic hide-and-seek—being revealed only after hearing the magical words, "Come out, come out, wherever you are!"

This question of God's residence or whereabouts is important. Some locate places of worship or denominational headquarters in close proximity to God's place. I remember once observing an abandoned, boarded-up church building in the inner city. On it was scrawled, "God don't live here no more!" I guess that's when God moved to the suburbs!

I've known of those who buy or build a house in order to be *closer* to God. Individuals have told me that God actually lives in Illinois—that is central Illinois. Others have said, no, it's southern Illinois. Still others have assured me it's Chicago!

I do sometimes get confused by the discussion of God's whereabouts. You see, it seems every place I've ever gone, God was there. Maybe God is actually like the rich and famous set with multiple residences. The way I travel about, I hope so!

God's Trust of Love

I recently heard a speaker say that every person requires at least seven hugs a day. I don't especially agree with that kind of formula. It seems too obligatory. However, it expresses the need of each person to experience human touch, the warmth of another human being. To be affirmed, not necessarily agreed with, and appreciated as a human being of value, beyond opinion or position, is a universal desire.

Speaking on love

In our culture, February is the time of year when we tell one another how much we love one another. Valentine's Day is boom time for the greeting card business.

In schools children will exchange their "I love you" greetings and come home with a bagful of such accolades.

I remember as a boy giving a Valentine to a special girl. Of course she didn't know she was special to me. As I grew older I also grew bolder, and a box of Valentine candy accompanied the card. Both were selected with great care and nervousness.

Special sweethearts give and receive expressions of their love or admiration. Husbands and wives make serious effort to find appropriate symbols of their love. Friends and associates take time to acknowledge how important they are to each other. It is a good day, a happy day for many, a sad day for some. As persons are reminded of their good fortune to know and experience love, others face the reality of its absence in their lives.

When Paul wrote the beautiful "love" chapter, the popular thirteenth chapter of I Corinthians, he could never imagine how important it would become in Christian thought. Surely he had no idea how many times it would be read in Christian and even non-religious weddings. How ironic that these words of a bachelor have such a prominent place in this significant ceremony.

Everyone needs to be loved and feel loved. The fact that many do not, even within their own families, is a sad commentary. Some have admitted they have gone through life never knowing love.

The meaning of love varies with nearly every user of the word. It is not always the same thing, not static but dynamic.

Perhaps that is our problem in talking about love, describing and experiencing it. Those who claim they are unloved or have never known love possibly are imagining one reality or expression of love while ignoring another.

My youngest sister always answers the telephone with the greeting, "Praise the Lord," and concludes our conversation with, "I love you!" Her words never cease to move me. They are not perfunctory but genuine.

Some people have difficulty saying "I love you." Others say it effortlessly. Thus the spoken words may lack meaning and have no reality or context.

I am certain that some people feel no need to say "I love you" because the love they have for a spouse, parent, child, or friend seems obvious. It does not need to be spoken. But that is only partially true.

The words must be heard as audible reminders of the reality. Others believe saying the words "I love you" replaces the reality of love. To say it is not to experience it! Experienced love makes real its audible expression. Love is active, not passive.

God loved the world so much that God did something about it! You love somebody somewhere—what will you do about it?

How to survive falling in and out of love

An often married and outspoken screen actress recently said, "It's as silly for a woman to divorce a man because she doesn't love him as it is to marry him because she does!" At first I considered it a frivolous statement, but as I unwrapped it, I found a profound truth.

What is the basis on which two people promise to spend the remainder of their lives together? And on what basis do they determine that life together is more unfulfilling than life apart?

June is the popular month for exchanging wedding vows. Some will be simple, others extravagant. Some couples will make their promises to each other in a courthouse, others in a church. Some weddings will be in private, others public. A recent wedding took place in a major league baseball stadium before the game!

Whatever the setting for this most significant covenant, a commonality runs through all of them. Almost without exception the couple who pledge their love and loyalty to each other expect that theirs is a lifetime commitment. Their feelings at that moment are so intense they can't imagine that these emotions will not be sustained through time. They believe that only death could separate them, for they have found in each other a wholeness that makes life more beautiful and meaningful.

I suppose many persons have been in love only once. Others fall in and out of love as often as the seasons change. How many times have you felt you were in love?

I was in love with at least one of my elementary school teachers, my high school English teacher, and my college music teacher! Of course, what I was experiencing and feeling was not love at all. In more serious places in life's journey, sometimes mature people can be as immature as was my love for those teachers who touched my life in profound ways.

A life together must be built on something stronger than how two people feel about each other. Physical attraction and social or family expectations will never sustain a relationship. To be in love, romantically speaking, is not a basis on which a marriage can survive.

An expert said something that caught my attention in an interesting discussion on interracial marriage. He observed, "It is not nearly as important to marry outside one's race as it is to marry outside one's philosophy of life."

Maybe people marry too quickly when they are in love and divorce just as quickly when they are "out of love." In both instances, more than love is required. Indeed, what is described as love in the first year of marriage is not what is meant by love in the twentieth, thirtieth, or fiftieth year.

There is no relationship like marriage. Not that it is higher, better, or more noble than others, but it is unique. It places two distinct lives in such close proximity that it makes both utterly vulnerable. They are seen by each other as no other sees them—warts and all. They must live together, promising to do so "until death do us part."

To make that kind of commitment one must be more than *in love*. Once made, it ought to take more than being *out of love* to break it.

When love comes again

They still act like newlyweds, although they have been married for a few years. Whenever I see them they are holding hands. She is effervescent with a twinkle in her eyes, he almost blushing and obviously in love with his "new" bride. Both are in their seventies, and each has lost a spouse to death.

As our population grows older we may see an ever-growing number of these "sunset year" marriages, couples who find each other after years of a happy marriage.

As death brings lifelong relationships to an end, many widows and widowers will feel that life has lost all meaning. Certainly no significant other will take the place of one who meant so much: the years together, children, grandchildren, perhaps great-grandchildren, memories. The years remaining may be lived alone; no spouse is desired or needed.

Then it happens! A man and a woman find love once more, different but nonetheless real, powerful, and meaningful. The words of promise are repeated once more, and the two become one.

Time is changing the attitudes of adult children and friends about sunset-year marriages. Children are becoming less protective and more understanding of the needs of a mother or father who has decided not to live alone after the death of a husband or wife. Friends don't look askance at such unions.

Frequently a widow or widower today is still in reasonably good health and continues an active life. New relationships will be formed. Love will blossom again and marriage will follow. That's good!

For those who find in another the qualities that will bring happiness in a life together, there is no need to deny such a relationship. It will not happen to everyone, but for those whom love visits twice, the sunset years can be as promising and happy as those years when age had not taken its toll.

"Til death us do part" are familiar words heard in most wedding ceremonies. Couples pledge to remain together through bad times as well as good, for better and for worse.

The covenant is made at a time when love seems invincible. But sadly, fewer marriages are enduring to the culmination of a partner's death. Many relationships can't sustain certain challenges. The bringing together of two complex personalities into such a demanding give-and-take relationship as marriage requires more than love. It requires commitment and hard work. Sometimes, for whatever reason, a couple or one partner is not willing to give what marriage requires.

The reasons some marriages fail are as varied as the couples. Broken relationships, marriages especially, are always painful. Realism has caused our Church to conclude, "Where marriage partners, even after thoughtful consideration and counsel, are estranged beyond reconciliation, we recognize divorce as regrettable but recognize the right of divorced persons to remarry."

Many find that love after divorce is possible. Sometimes the pain of a broken marriage is so great and the disappointment so strong that remarriage seems out of the question.

Then without plan or expectation, love comes again.

I rejoice for couples who find love and relationship after loss and brokenness. The Church has said, "We encourage an active, accepting, and enabling commitment of the church in our society to minister to members of divorced and remarried families" (Para. 71D, *The Book of Discipline* of The United Methodist Church).

When one finds love the second time around, and that is culminated in a loving wholesome marriage, it is a gift.

Fatherhood with a kiss and a tear

We've just sent our third daughter away to college. I thought it would be easier this time; it wasn't. I am one of those doting fathers who makes a fuss over his daughters and takes issue with those who hold that tenderness, affection, and a loving relationship are exclusively and innately maternal instincts. Fathers, as well as mothers, can be and often are loving, caring parents.

Leaving our daughter at a dormitory, where she would make new friends and begin another phase of life without us, was more difficult than I anticipated. I postponed departing as long as I could, but then I saw that "don't you think it's time for you to leave" look in my daughter's eye. I caught the not too subtle hint and left her room. She wouldn't even walk to the parking lot with us! After a quick parting kiss we walked to the car alone.

My wife, Kim, said in her smug New England air, "Okay, Woodie, you can cry now." She insists that I have cried after each of our daughters went away to college. Actually, it was only coincidental that on both previous occasions I got something in my eyes that caused them to water.

While parenting is an increasingly difficult task, it also holds many joys. Loving, caring, and shaping the lives of children are important responsibilities. To think that God trusted us with these tender lives is humbling, and the complexity of the task in this new age is challenging. Parents seem to exercise less control and influence than in years gone by, but I refuse to abdicate that responsibility entrusted to me by a wise and generous God.

I'm no ideal dad, and I have made my share of parental goofs. I'm possibly too demanding on the one hand and too lenient on the other. I must plead guilty to having spent less time with my children than they had a right to expect, but I showered them with love and have spoiled them—healthily, I hope!

At a time when there seems to be so much news about child abuse—physical, emotional, and sexual—I pause and wonder how it's possible to bruise these special ones. Parental neglect and abuse are especially painful and puzzling to me. I ponder what the underlying causes are for such abuse. We are fortunate to have many organizations and groups to help parents who have succumbed to such behavior, and I hope that more parents seek the help that is available. I am encouraged by the efforts of organizations dedicated to ensuring that appropriate laws, policies, and programs are available for the protection and well-being of our children. Our children are our future, and they are our present.

Responsible parenthood is also a stewardship concern. Having been given the capability and opportunity to bring life into the world is only half the story; the other half is the responsibility to care for and nurture that life so it becomes a blessing to the world. God expects it of us who have been given the privilege of parenting. We are not expected to be perfect parents, whatever that is, but we are expected to be responsible, caring, loving, guiding, and correcting. The hard reality is that we parents can never ensure what will be the outcome of our efforts. We can only hope, pray, and trust, but there is a sense of accomplishment when we know we've done our best—or almost.

As we walked back to our car that beautiful Sunday afternoon, I looked at the lovely campus, manicured lawn, and stately buildings. Then I looked up at my daughter's dorm and into her window, took a deep breath, and it happened again—I got something in my eye!

The power of love

Now I am a grandfather! It did not happen as I dreamed, hoped, or wished. It is bittersweet.

I am not the first parent met with the news of a pending birth under such unfavorable circumstances. But this realization brings no comfort. I can't believe the adage "Misery loves company." No other parent should be visited with the pain, disappointment, and frustration the months have forced me to bear. I wondered how I would survive the heavy burden.

The days and nights were filled with anxiety, anger, and regret. I prayed and wept, then wept and prayed. So much raced through my tired and troubled mind. Most thoughts were not noble and are best left between God and me.

Why? was the recurring question. I searched for answers, but few came. I longed for the power to control others' lives and decisions, but knew it was futile. When relating to adults, one can finally control only one's own life. On most days that is about all I can manage.

The struggle continues. My principles and ideals will not be compromised, surrendered, or rationalized away, whatever the circumstances. Therefore, I choose to live with ambiguity.

So often in life we face a single problem, awesome in its impact. Because it appears to be catastrophic we deny it, try to run from it, or by unwise actions create two problems where there was one. It gets out of hand so easily and quickly. Soon our problem has problems. I resist this human inclination.

Somehow the resources to deal with this latest jolt to life and the shattering of dreams would be found. And they came: in the strength and steadiness of a devoted wife, in the love of four children undergirded by a tenacious sense of forgiveness and grace, in God who sustains even in moments of deep despair, and in a beloved community that when trusted demonstrates its caring and support. But it is still not easy.

The moment arrived when I held my two-day-old grandson in my arms and embraced tightly my precious and vulnerable daughter. I knew then as I know now something of the power of love and the gift of life. So small and doll-like was he as I gazed into his sleeping face. How peaceful he looked, how trusting. Immediately this inexplicable special love, which always emerges when things happen in life requiring the extraordinary, overtook me. He will need it. As long as I have life I shall give it.

My daughter, too, will need that extra touch of grace. Through my disappointment and concern will flow more abundantly my unending love. She must be assured that the quality of my love for her is not measured by what she does or does not accomplish, or if she pleases or displeases me.

I have this unique opportunity to demonstrate the meaning of love and grace about which she has so often heard me preach. I will risk that love's being misinterpreted or even abused, but I will love anyway.

I shall shower my grandson, Bryan Michael, with affection and attention. I shall tell him that how he started life is not nearly as important as what he contributes to life. He will be special as all God's children are special: not because of where or to whom they are born, where they live or how they look, but because they belong to a good and loving God. I will remind him.

Now I have a grandson. I wonder what he will be when he grows up. I hope he will be kind.

What color is love?

The religious periodical comes to our home regularly. I didn't realize my daughter read it until her comment came with unquestionable candor and considerable emotion.

"I disagree with this!" she exclaimed. She pointed to a printed announcement in the periodical.

The announcement under the handsome picture of a cute little fellow with big eyes and a broad smile read, "Wanted: A black family to adopt this child."

My daughter and I had a good discussion. I like playing the role of antagonist in our family. I almost always take the opposite position in most discussions. The family knows it. In fact I think they now expect it. It makes for good family interaction. So I pushed my daughter pretty hard about this delicate and emotional issue. However, we were not discussing some esoteric intellectual proposition or remote philosophical issue. We were talking about a human being, a young boy named Harold, who wanted and needed a home, a place of love and security. That's serious!

The issue is sometimes referred to as transracial, cross-cultural, or cross-racial adoption. It describes the practice of adoption by a family of one race a child of a different racial or ethnic background. In some communities and among certain professional groups it is a very controversial issue.

As I have observed the practice, it usually involves a white family or couple who adopts a child who is black, Hispanic, Native American, or Asian American. Increasingly, it may involve a child from Asia; the adoption of children from Korea seems especially popular.

The most volatile debate, however, involves the adoption of a black child by a white family. Celebrated court cases have involved such adoption disputes.

Approximately twenty years ago at a national family life conference, I led a workshop for couples who had adopted children across racial lines. It was a heart-wrenching and candid session, with many leaving wondering if they had made the right decision and others affirming their decision.

I've read the rulings of judges on both sides of the issue. Some concluded that children were ill-served by such an adoption, and others ruled that these adoptions were clearly in the best interest of the child.

I have listened to those who grew up in such homes and heard their stories of adjustment woes and identity conflict. Especially sad were those involving black children living in a white family in an all white community. Racism in America has a special pathos in its black/white dimensions. However, I've noted also those whose experiences are characterized more by love than trauma.

There are those blacks and whites who oppose cross-racial adoption on the premise of "protecting the race." Such arguments continue with varying intensity.

In the meantime, Harold and hundreds like him need and want a home, sometimes unaware of the idea of race, which has such significant impact on their lives. They continue to move from one foster home to another or from one child-care institution to another. Some are caring places, others not. But is the most caring institution a preferable substitute for a permanent, loving, nurturing home where parents understand the possible risks and pitfalls of cross-racial adoption and equip themselves responsibly to meet them head on, and who are capable of helping their child to do the same?

I wish for every child to know the security of a nurturing and loving home.

Wanted: A family who will love Harold and give him the strength and sustenance to face life and become a blessing to the world.

The touch of One who cares

It had been a dreadful week, one of those in which I was certain my instincts not to become a bishop should have been heeded! I sat at my desk with correspondence to answer, reports to read, and telephone messages to return. Then a pastor who had no appointment was suddenly in our office asking to see me. He entered with a broad grin. I rose to greet him and extended my hand, which he thoroughly ignored. Instead he gave me the warmest hug one could imagine and said, "I know it's rough, but I just wanted to tell you you're doing a good job!" I was shocked!

Somewhat embarrassed, he assured me his intent was not to butter me up. He didn't want anything, he said, except to let me know that I was appreciated. He left just as suddenly as he had appeared.

My trusted and faithful secretary commented, "What a thoughtful gesture." For me it was more than a gesture; it was a gift sent from heaven. I did not need the words as much as I needed the hug, the act of caring, the touch of one beggar to another beggar, a soul embrace that transcends opinion and difference. It was a hug that found me in my moment of need. Nothing can take the place of human touch.

Studies have been made of controlled groups of newborn infants who were observed in order to determine factors that affected their development. Both groups were carefully given the same environmental context, proper care and feeding, excellent medical attention, and secure surroundings. But one group of infants received more hugs, cuddling, and kisses. The study showed that the infants who were touched more proved to be less irritable, better adjusted, and had fewer health problems. Touch nurtures the spirit.

The increase of child abuse has resulted in more caution among many adults in relating to children. Unfortunately, those who work with children—teachers, day-care attendants, even family members—have reduced to a minimum the touching of children, including their own.

Children have learned to be more cautious of those who touch them. It is a sad state of affairs, understandable but nevertheless unfortunate. Pastors, too, have been reminded to be more cautious in outward displays of affection toward parishioners of the opposite sex.

Today many adults struggle with their inability to express warmth and affection because, as they report, they experienced so little in their homes. I have heard of those who cannot recall ever being hugged or kissed by a mother or father. They lack the assuring embrace or tender touch of parent.

I recently heard a speaker say that every person requires at least seven hugs a day. I don't especially agree with that kind of formula. It seems too obligatory. However, it expresses the need of each person to experience human touch, the warmth of another human being. To be affirmed, not necessarily agreed with, and appreciated as a human being of value, beyond opinion or position, are universal desires.

Some are afraid of the intimacy involved in a hug. Others find it difficult to overcome a lifetime of deprivation and socialization that discouraged intimacy or the expression of emotion. Their need for touch is no less profound.

The well-known gospel songwriter William J. Gaither has written a popular tune, "He Touched Me." It tells of the soul's delight in the touch of the Master. Guilt and shame are relieved, acceptance and wholeness experienced. Something happens in that divine touch that causes the heart and soul to soar.

Many can attest to such an experience when touched by the Lord of life. To know that touch is matchless. But that is not the only touch needed in our faith journey. We also need the touch of a loved one, colleague, friend, even adversary. Someone is waiting for your touch and needing your hug today. It can make a difference.

Mysteries of Life and Death

That emptiness is made full again when in the agony of prayer no words come, clichés are forgotten, pretense abandoned; then the cry of the soul is more eloquent than any spoken words. And you recover the power of prayer that is not in the petition but in the grace of One who gives even before you ask. You realize how truly insignificant are your words and how mighty is the God who does not need your words; your emptiness is enough.

The joy and tears of Christmas

There is a universal character to Christmas.

While traditions and customs differ from place to place, this important day and season of the Christian year possess a commonality and sameness. The focus of the Christ child, a spirit of hope, and expressions of goodwill are some of the elements found in the celebration of Christmas, whatever its context. It is a season of joy.

Christmas, however, is unique. It is contextual. Each of us has our special memories and meanings of the season. It is deeply personal—our very own. Like a fingerprint, it belongs to no one else. It may appear the same, but it is not.

Christmas is the season of joy, but ironically it is also a season of sadness and tears. Sometimes the sadness is camouflaged by the joyous activities, the laughter and gaiety. Yet the tears must be shed in quick moments snatched between laughter and frivolity.

Christmas is a season of gathering and remembering; herein are both its joy and sadness. We remember the Savior's coming in human form to make God known to all the people. It is a time of singing because he has come into the world to change history and into one's heart to change life.

Each Christian sings his or her own personal song of Christmas. The full text of the song is known only to God and the singer.

It is a time of remembering the Savior and of recalling Christmases past and loved ones dear.

Christmas in its special way reveals one's own mortality. In the midst of the season and its joy one sees self—young and childlike, yet mature and growing older.

Perhaps this is in part the reason for melancholy and tears

amidst the joy. Family and loved ones gather and experience gratitude and thanksgiving in their presence. Yet their very presence makes the absence of other dear ones so poignant. Some are separated by miles, others by broken relationships or death.

During the Christmas season we are reminded of our frailty and brokenness. Those who are alone seem lonelier, the broken heart more broken. Hurt seems to hurt more at Christmas.

So it is the season of a strange mixture for many, moving back and forth from merriment to melancholy, laughter to tears.

The tears of Christmas are not all of sadness, for they are also tears of joy. So at Christmas, when the incongruity of "Merry Christmas" and tears mingle, each will have its own meaning and its own memories.

A mother's faith speaks

I looked into her eyes, void of tears, exhausted with weeping. I expected rage and found none. I gently touched her hand. She clasped mine with strength, yet need.

This remarkable mother was waiting to lead the funeral procession into the church for the service to commemorate the life of her daughter, who, only in her early twenties, had been tragically shot and killed.

Also shot in the same incident that gripped our community was a second daughter, a high school student, who remained in a coma. How could the mother bear it? I thought. Yet she, who had every right to be overcome with grief and anger, seemed so composed.

I often wonder about those who meet tragedy of colossal proportions. I tried to imagine myself in the place of this mother and was sick just with the thought.

At the close of the moving and tearful service the mother moved to the pulpit, accompanied by her pastor. The congregation looked shocked. How could she make a statement? With one lovely daughter dead and another lingering close to death, how could she call up enough strength and faith to address those gathered in this place of overwhelming sadness?

She spoke with deliberateness and assurance. No self-pity, no question of "Why did this happen to me?" Instead this United Methodist Christian spoke of love, responsibility, hope, and community.

I no longer fought back the tears; I needed the release. Hundreds had gathered to comfort her. As she spoke she was bringing comfort to this congregation of young and old, all bewildered.

I am captivated by this woman of such inner strength. I think of her almost daily. This mother has such obvious faith and depth. Her heart surely is torn, her nights long, and pain deep. I still see her eyes, remember her touch, recall her words.

Every May we can be sure that we will be reminded to remember mothers. They will be celebrated and praised, gifted and pampered. Calls will be made, prayers raised, and songs sung to their honor. But this year I will remember in a special way this remarkable mother who has briefly but profoundly touched my life.

For others whose lives have been interrupted by tragedy, Mother's Day may have some poignant and painful reminders and moments. Yet in the midst of such moments, may they somehow sense their value and the love and appreciation that may too often go unexpressed.

Everyone deserves to be cared for, remembered

I had never given much thought to the possibility of dying alone. My thoughts instead have centered on the bereaved who are mourning the death of a loved one. Expressions of sympathy come to those experiencing loss, bewilderment, and sometimes anger. We try to comfort those who mourn.

It was something of a jolt when the report crossed my desk. In it I read that literally thousands die and are neither mourned or missed. These persons, often indigent or living alone, are taken to a city or county morgue. Their remains are never claimed.

A report indicates that in Cook County, Illinois, twenty persons on the average are buried each month after their remains have gone unclaimed or unidentified for about a two-month period. They have either lived in such a way as to have lost all contact with friends or loved ones, or those who know them do not have the means, time, or interest to offer an appropriate burial. It is sad.

Imagine living in such a way that no one cares if you live or die. Or reflect on outliving friends and family and having no one to remember or care.

A part of one's immortality is to be remembered. I still remember those who in some way touched my life, who made me laugh or cry, dream and hope. I recall the emptiness and loss I felt when their lives came to an end. Something in me died too, but something of them lived on in me as well.

Healing happens in the community gathered to worship and remember. We cry, but we often laugh, and always we remember the one in whose memory we have come together. We offer prayers for strength, comfort, and thanksgiving for that person's life.

Life should not be so discarded that no one remembers, no one cares, no one offers prayers, no one sheds tears. I wonder about those whose remains are never identified or claimed. What went wrong? Whom did they fail or who failed them? Probably at some point they were in a Sunday school class, a member of a church, in a family. Some, of course, never had the undergirding of a loving home and a caring church, so they died as they lived—with utter loneliness and rejection. Too many see life and death from this underside. It causes one to wonder about the fairness of it all.

So I grieve for those who have no one to grieve for them. And I pray for those who have rejected loved ones, vowing to disown them forever—in life and even in death! No deed seems so dastardly as to deserve such rejection.

Our lives ought to count for something. Most of us will not be famous. No books will be written about us, no monuments erected to our memory. But we should live in meaningful ways that will make a difference. Someone should weep at our passing or smile when they remember laughs we brought to others. We should be missed if only for a little while. Something should have happened on earth that would not have occurred without us. Life should remember us.

It is said, "To live and die alone is a human tragedy, but not to be remembered and mourned . . . after earthly life . . . is an ugly blemish on human dignity." So to thousands who lived and died alone, for whom no one grieved, cared, or remembered, the one consolation is that God cared and God wept.

The blues song of the night

The blues singer reaches to the depths of the soul and cries out in song, "Help me make it through the night!" It is not clear to whom the appeal is made; the listener hears only the agony and desperation.

Night is mysterious and foreboding. Darkness falls, and what was seen so vividly during the day is hidden. On the other hand, the hidden or the submerged during the day becomes overwhelmingly evident during the dark of night. What is there about night that causes feelings of despair to intensify, hurt to hurt more, loneliness to be more lonely?

Many early cultures and societies have had nighttime rituals to still the evil spirits that roamed during night. Night seems to be the time most welcomed by evil. The legendary Count Dracula comes alive and stalks his victims by night but must return to the grave before daybreak. Daylight is not kind to evil; night sustains it!

A quiet house in daytime somehow produces strange and unusual sounds in the darkness. They are night sounds. Longfellow has mused, "How absolute and omnipotent is the silence of night! And yet the stillness seems almost audible."

I often wonder if there is any correlation between death and night. How many die at night compared to day? Is there some sense in which the body's defenses surrender more easily in darkness, the will is less determined? I wonder if more suicides take place at night. What is there about night? Perhaps it is the stillness: fewer distractions to help one avoid realities or ward off illusions. No activity distracts; one simply must be rather than do, must listen rather than speak.

I suppose the death of a loved one, a spouse, for example, is more unbearable at night when nothing remains but memories, silence, and loneliness. Heartbreak is heavier at night. One rehearses what might have been and in the stillness contemplates what has so successfully been avoided in daylight.

Many parents still use nightlights to provide enough wattage to break the darkness. Some children, when they discover darkness, seem to have a natural fear of it. Others never overcome it, or at least its discomfort follows into adulthood. Some simply refuse to sleep without benefit of light.

Night can be so long! No wonder the heart sings, "Help me make it through the night!" The hours move slowly, lingering for what seems an eternity. Constructive contemplation gives way to unproductive imaginings. Praying helps—sometimes, but it often seems more drudgery than relief. Somewhere in all this pain and bewilderment the Christian reaches for God, knowing that the God of light is also the God of darkness. There is the hope, the assurance, that if only one can survive these hours, this utter darkness, surely God must know; and the words now become a hymn of petition, "Help me make it through the night."

Sometimes, you know not when, eyelids close and whatever burden that had been carried—fear, pain, exhaustion, guilt, frustration, anxiety, or loneliness—leaves and sleep comes, if only momentarily.

Or perhaps you venture to outwait night, seated at a table with a cup of coffee, pacing the floor, or just lying there, hoping and knowing you will win this battle with night. Then in the darkness light breaks through ever so gently and faintly. The night becomes pregnant with light, and you strain less now to see it. The once darkened room becomes brighter, and you glimpse the faint blue sky or the hint of a sunrise. With fatigue and relief you know that you have indeed made it through the night. God heard!

Awaiting death is burden and blessing

They are waiting for her to die. It is certain she will; only the exact time is unknown. It could be months, weeks, days, or even hours.

She is so young that it seems unfair. It is unfair! The family shows remarkable endurance, and so does she, but she is tired. The doctors have done their best. Medicines and surgery have exhausted their capabilities, and indeed now body and mind say, "No more!" The pain is too great, the effort too futile, the conclusion too inevitable.

Like sudden and unexpected death, awaiting death has its peculiar pain. It drags the process out and, in a sense, all who wait are dying a little. It is draining, financially, emotionally, spiritually.

It is so hard for the children. The young have not garnered sufficient emotional fortitude for death; to them it is something far off in another community or on television, not in their home. There are basketball games, studying, exams, and dating. And now this awful intrusion: Death lingers, and they must watch and wait. They pray with a passion normally associated with those more mature and advanced in years.

Somehow life must necessarily go on, activity must be normalized. Yet to wait for death is an abnormal time; it calls for every ounce of resolve. Whence will it come?

Everyone seems to have at least a twinge of guilt. The one who waits to be taken knows how demanding the ordeal is on loved ones in terms of cost, time, and energy. All of this could be put to better use, and so there is a sense of guilt.

Those who wait get tired even in the midst of their sorrow. They want to go on to other chapters in life, but this seems callous and stirs up guilt. Everyone wishes he or she had been more kind, more considerate, had taken more time to enjoy life. Wishes bring guilt because time is running out.

Somewhere in the process God is blamed, if not for causing events, at least for not interceding and making things better. Guilt emerges from this seeming blasphemy.

Awaiting death, however, allows for preparation, which is

both good and bad. When grief is minimal and thinking clearer, appropriate arrangements can be made. Yet there is a kind of awkwardness about it when the death has not yet died. The waiting gives an opportunity to say all those things that would never have been said without this extraordinary time: The "I love you's" and "I'm sorry—forgive me," are too often left unsaid. It's a time to hold hands when no words are necessary, to read or sit or just be present. These are the paradoxical gifts of awaiting death.

The time is an opportunity to get it right with God, the encounter of faith with existential reality. No slick theological propositions and high-sounding jargon, no colleagues to impress, just you and God talking it over, sometimes in anger and despair, fear and uncertainty, but always in hope and assurance. Tears are inevitable.

Awaiting death could devastate and sometimes does. Somehow, though, the Christian must remember that the waiting is not alone. Family and loved ones wait together. In a remarkable way strength is shared; when one is down another is up. When one is weak, the strength is supplied by still another. So often the one who waits for death to claim him or her miraculously brings relief to those who mourn. In the midst of it all is this peculiar Christian certainty that God waits with us. No moment, day, or hour exists when we are utterly alone.

Fledglings give lessons on death and life

The youngsters were excited. My wife, Kim, a first-grade teacher, decided to illustrate a special unit she was teaching by having her class observe ten eggs go through incubation; she hoped that ten baby chicks would hatch. The eggs were placed in the incubator where they received proper light and temperature and were rotated carefully each day. Every morning for weeks the children came to class excitedly—expecting, watching, hoping.

After weeks of waiting, one by one the shells were cracked. The little chicks were pecking away and breaking the wall that had held them. The children were ecstatic; so was their teacher. The whole school was now caught up in this drama taking place in Mrs. White's room.

But one chick was having difficulty. It couldn't quite break through; it seemed trapped, weak, or both. The children and their teacher were concerned. Kim gently and carefully assisted in cracking the shell and enabling the chick to complete the process and free itself. It obviously was not as strong and lively as the others. The children were still concerned.

In this lesson on life the teacher tried to prepare the class for the worst. In choosing her words carefully to explain the baby chick's difficulty, she instructed the children that the chick could be sick. Then one youngster said in a clear strong voice, "Mrs. White, do you mean the chick might die?" She was startled by the straightforwardness of the question/statement.

The youngster and perhaps others were more prepared to deal with that possibility than the teacher anticipated. Somehow in their six-year-old world, some had come to know something about death. How much, of course, is a question, but at least one little boy knew the language and reality and called it by name!

Sometimes it is difficult even for adults to call death by name. We find other words that are more evasive, more gentle to describe the reality—words such as "to pass away," "loss," "the other side." The words "death" and "die" seem too harsh, perhaps too final, even morbid.

"Mrs. White, do you mean the chick might die?" There's the question—stark, real. Doctor, do you mean it's terminal? Do you mean I might die? Is there no hope? Do you mean she might die? Even the most faithful ones among us at times avoid the reality of our own death or that of a loved one or cherished friend. We can't even fully contemplate the question about our own mortality and death. Some avoid as much as possible all that would confirm it: the preparing of the will, the funeral service, and all else that would make more evident the fact that "Yes, I'm going to die!"

It's natural. It's normal. We don't like to contemplate death. I notice how quickly my daughters change the subject when I remind them of my mortality. Their eyes drop, and I know what they're thinking: "Dad, don't talk like that." When you're a teenager death is not a part of your world. But even as one grows older, ways are found, futilely I'm afraid, to avoid the reality of death.

The ways in which death comes are sometimes tragic, senseless, and inexplicable, but the reality of death is a part of God's created order. Life and death go hand in hand. There will always be some mystery about death, as there is mystery about life, but it is inevitable. To give undue attention to death and dwell on it can be morbid. To ignore it, however, is irresponsible and futile. Death comes to us all; it is the most democratic reality I know. The mystery is how and why it comes as it does, not that it will come. It will come!

"Mrs. White, do you mean the chick might die?" What would you say to a first-grader?

Giving way to tears can be a blessing

In a presidential campaign some years ago, one of the prominent candidates wept briefly during an emotional moment. It was not a sustained or hysterical outpouring of tears but a momentary expression of grief, sorrow, and disappointment.

Although the candidate had distinguished himself in government service for almost his entire adult life, his public tears became a media event and were used as proof that he did not have what it takes to govern a nation. Soon his front-runner status was threatened, and eventually he was declared not a viable candidate for president. One might say he lost the opportunity to be president of the United States because he shed a few tears in public.

I once heard a rather negative evaluation of a pastor because "he cried too easily." Women politicians and candidates for political office are especially scrutinized to determine if they display that sign of gender "weakness," tears that come too easily! Tears, signs of weakness in our culture, are also considered unmasculine. We assure little girls that it is all right to cry; after all they are the "weaker" sex. We chide and warn little boys that "boys don't cry."

Yet tears have a ministry! Perhaps we would all be better off if we wept more. Tears express both joy and sorrow; to suppress either could diminish joy and sustain grief.

A *Washington Post* article, "Tears: An Enduring Mystery" by Curt Suplee, caught my attention. It summarizes findings and research being done by scientists and medical researchers on the nature of tears. The writer indicates that the eye produces "three slightly different" kinds of tears: "continuous tears," "reflex tears," and "emotional or psychogenic tears." The latter category includes those we refer to as tears of sadness or joy.

Of interest is one finding in a fifteen-year study on tears in which the researchers have conjectured, "The reason people feel better after crying is that they may be removing, in their tears, chemicals that build up during emotional stress."

The stress may literally be emptying itself through tears. There may be not only psychological and spiritual benefits from shedding tears but physiological ones as well.

I recently learned of a rare disease called alacrima. This renders a person unable to cry because the body cannot manufacture the necessary fluids to produce tears. Imagine not being able to cry! Yet many persons have a kind of self-imposed alacrima. They can't, won't, and refuse to cry even in their special place of privacy.

I have not escaped totally the socialization process, but I have not lost the ability to cry. Sometimes I fear I cry too easily. Tears come during a great musical work or the singing of a hymn, during a drama, and even a sunrise. They come from tragic news reports of famine, earthquakes, bombings, or airplane crashes. Tears come at the hearing of good news and bad—birth and death.

While expected to control public tears, I won't allow society to rob me of my private tears; they are a source of healing, cleansing, and renewal.

I trust that you too have discovered that tears can be a friend, and that you will remember the words of Jesus, who said, "Blessed are you who weep" (Luke 6:21 NRSV).

On filling our empty place

I think it happens to more people than is commonly recognized—a sense of emptiness. The spirit seems to be null and void. There is nothing to sustain and especially nothing to give.

Emptiness. Somehow the spoken words don't connect with that inner self and source that gives meaning and substance to the words. Acts, however noble, don't strike any note of satisfaction or fulfillment. That place in every heart that makes life sing seems to be asleep or absent.

So people fake it. At least some do. They go through the motions and make believe so none will know or suspect how empty life is for them. Those on whom others depend greatly go into a kind of automatic pilot; something in the psyche recalls all the appropriate responses—words, actions, motions. They keep going but are empty nonetheless.

Others just collapse. Frustrated, they are unable to cope. They can't even recall enough meaning in the past to sustain them in the present. They can't give to life because they simply feel there is nothing to give.

Emptiness is like a desert place, dry and barren and lonely, but for the Christian it should be a temporary place only, a passing-through place.

How is our empty place made full again? Fortunately, we are not the source of the refilling, for we are not smart enough, strong enough, or courageous enough to replenish the empty places. But there is a Source available to every weary, bruised, lonely, and empty soul.

He comes to us in so many ways: through worship, for instance. There the community of believers gathers in song and praise to recall the divine initiative of God's love for the people, come uniquely in Jesus Christ. As they sing songs of faith, raise their prayers, and hear the Word preached, the fullness of the Spirit replenishes the emptiness of the soul.

Jesus comes in those still and quiet moments when we wait for his presence to overwhelm us with such undeniable power that the soul knows it has been reunited with the Source of its strength and meaning. "Be still and know that I am God."

That emptiness is made full again when in the agony of prayer no words come, cliches are forgotten, pretense abandoned; then the cry of the soul is more eloquent than any spoken words. And you recover the power of prayer that is not in the petition but in the grace of One who gives even before you ask. You realize how truly insignificant are your words and how mighty is the God who does not need your words; your emptiness is enough.

Fullness comes in the touch of a loved one or the word of a stranger who without even intending fills your empty place. Or it comes as someone listens to your cries and sometimes has answers but often has only the ability, time, and caring to listen.

If only we could remember in our emptiness that we are not alone and recall the assurance of the words of the old spiritual, "trouble don't last always."

My empty place is made full every time I read the words of Isaiah: "But those who wait for the Lord shall renew their strength, they shall mount up with wings like eagles, they shall run and not be weary, they shall walk and not faint" (Isaiah 40:31 NRSV).

How my soul rejoices that emptiness is just a temporary place.

Each of us can be the answer to someone else's loneliness

When she came toward me I thought I detected a smile on her face, but then the smile turned to sadness as she sobbed, "I'm so lonely!" I was caught totally by surprise. She is normally so cheery, talkative, even playful. She is a widow and now in her seventies.

"I'm so lonely!" There was not much I could do but listen. No words could change her feelings. She soon got it all out, dried her tears, and our conversation turned to something else. But inwardly now I was weeping, for I knew shortly she would return to her home, to its memories, and to silence.

Millions of people make up what is referred to as single-member households. Some are never-married young adults, others divorcees; there are those in between singleness and marriage. Many have chosen the single life and find in it fulfillment and freedom. Many are in what is often referred to as the twilight years: retired, widowed, living alone. Many are active, enjoying reasonably good health and independence. But I am certain, in spite of their activeness and independence, they have many moments of loneliness.

Although the lonely feelings of the elderly are accentuated as they observe and experience a changing time as loved ones and friends pass away, or the familiar replaced with the new, there are others also who experience loneliness.

Other single adults may be inadvertently left out of planning, programs, activities. Because so many are young and active, we often assume that they are busy with more invitations than they can accept. In our family- and couple-oriented society they can become invisible, especially in church programs and activities.

In coming years we shall experience an unprecedented number of single adults. One phenomenon United Methodism faces is an increasing number of single clergy. I'm not sure that the denomination and congregation are adequately prepared to deal with this phenomenon or are fully aware of its implications. Every human being has the need to feel wanted, accepted, loved, and appreciated. Nothing can replace a meaningful relationship. To be fully human is to react to and be touched by others in the human family.

How many others are there who experience but fail to articulate their sense of loneliness? I imagine they are in our congregations, among our clergy and other professional church leadership, in the office or factory, on the farm or down the street, in the classroom or on the campus.

Is there someone waiting for your visit or telephone call? A card or letter reminding a loved one or friend that she or he is remembered and loved can be just what the doctor ordered. An invitation to dinner or a cup of coffee with one who lives alone might brighten a day otherwise spent in gloom.

A weekend away from the silence of a house or apartment could make it more bearable. For some, to hear the laughter and see little children at play might rekindle memories of days more full and joyous. These are small but significant ways that the people of God can reach out to one another, touching lives and souls and making life more meaningful.

In James Weldon Johnson's moving poem "Creation," when God has finished all of creation, God says, "I'm lonely still. . . ." Then God creates the human family!

Yes, we are the answer to one another's loneliness—not things or possessions, not meaningless activities, but interaction between human beings—flesh to flesh, heart to heart, soul to soul.

Whose life do you need to touch today?

I had a dream

It was the worst Christmas of my life.

The telephone rang about 7:00 A.M. Christmas morning; the concerned caller wanted to verify the message he had just received that a mutual friend had died. Ridiculous, I exclaimed; I had received no such call, and I'd just seen him two days before. I decided to call my friend, wish him a merry Christmas, and laugh with him about the rumor of his death.

No sooner had I put the receiver down than the telephone rang with the news: My friend had indeed died of a massive heart attack on Christmas Eve while he and his family watched the telecast of the *Nutcracker Suite.* I went back to bed and remained there all day.

Nearly a year following my friend's death I had the following dream: I had just gotten onto the subway at Washington National Airport. As I stepped into the subway car, I was astonished to see my friend through the glass door in the next car. He was not dead after all; it was just a cruel joke. I waved to him and he to me, then he beckoned me.

Dreams are strange bits of unreality and reality, but somehow I was able to get off the subway train, which was still at the station. I ran to a telephone, called my friend's wife to tell her that I had found him. He was not dead after all; I would bring him home. Then I dashed back onto the waiting train.

He was still standing in the next car. His face beamed with that familiar smile. How I rejoiced that my friend was alive! The train lurched and began to move. I quickly opened the door to the adjoining car where my friend was, only to discover as I entered that he was in the next one. He stood there smiling, not saying anything.

The train increased its speed. I stumbled through the aisle to the door connecting the next car where my friend stood. Now I was calling his name at the top of my voice. "George! George!" I entered the car; he was not there but in the next! This went on for some time; in each subway car I discovered my friend ahead in another.

The train slowed and soon stopped, but the car in which my friend was riding detached itself from the rest of the train. I was still calling his name; he still stood there smiling. His car continued to move away—farther and farther, faster and faster. It was nearly out of sight. I called out to my friend, now through sobs. I could scarcely see him; the smile was fading. Soon the subway car was totally out of sight. My friend was gone! Now I knew he was never coming back.

Then I awoke and I heard myself saying, "Okay, God. Okay."

Celebrations of Caring

Everyone ought to have a special someone, a person with whom he or she can laugh and cry, share fears and doubts, joys and sorrows, that special someone who knows, understands, and loves us anyway.

When we feel alone, we hear words that break through the loneliness and give us a sense of belonging or acceptance—a simple word, such as friend.

Letting go is never easy

"She is too young to go to the prom, and besides, she's my baby!"

My reaction, when confronted recently with the request of my youngest daughter, a sophomore, to attend the high school prom, put me typically on the opposing, losing side of family discussion. Is it more difficult to be a father or a bishop? No one should have to be both simultaneously.

I gave in! Among a long list of conditions was that we get acquainted with the young man who had invited my daughter to the prom. I would also have to check into his background through my special sources. He passed!

Great care and love went into the making by her mother of a beautiful green dress with two pink bows. Although I surprised our daughter with a simple pink pearl necklace and earrings, I was still not enthusiastic about the prospects of my baby going out with a young man who was probably more mature and worldly wise.

Her date arrived, handsome in tails and pink bow tie and matching cummerbund, a corsage in hand. Our family members' giving him the once-over obviously increased his nervousness. I tried to put him at ease, and then I reminded him of the time he should have my daughter home. A sharp look from my wife was clearly a deserved reprimand.

Then coming down the stairs, with "oohs and aahs" from the family, was not my little girl but a young woman, growing up before my very eyes. I hadn't noticed.

She even walked different despite her self-consciousness, held her head high as though she had practiced. Indoors and outdoors we took pictures of this young, nervous couple. More than once they were urged to get closer—not by me, of course! "Smile, don't look so somber," was another direction.

After they drove off for a memorable night in my daughter's life—her first prom—I stood at the window long after the car was out of sight. I thought about nothing in particular, yet everything. Where has the time gone? She was only ten years old when we came here. Shy, quiet, she's growing into a lovely young lady. Somehow I thought it would take longer; maybe it was just my wishful thinking.

Perhaps I will never quite see our daughter again as I once saw her, not after remembering the sight of this lovely young lady descending the stairs in a formal evening gown, a touch of makeup on, and a gleam in her eye that I had never seen before.

Spring is the season of letting go—turning loose—saying good-byes and farewells. Weddings and graduations, while they mark a beginning, also represent an ending. Closure. In a strange way prom night will represent that for many parents and children.

Letting go is not easy for a parent who loves a child, a congregation who admires a pastor, or a pastor who has nurtured a congregation. It is nonetheless a part of life. I pray that I shall learn to do it more gracefully.

Friends are for loving

Three United Methodist ministers and their spouses drove more than ten hours. Our daughters thought it unusual that these friends would drive so far, at great expense and time, to spend with us what actually was less time than that required to drive to Illinois and return to a neighboring state.

We had so little time together. The demands of schedule and calendar prevented a longer period. We gathered around the dining room table and talked for hours. We reminisced and shared about families, children, ministry, and the church. We talked into the wee hours about joys and sorrows. We laughed a lot.

Our lives together began as we entered theological school and continued as we became pastors and spouses and parents. While serving together in the same geographical area, we met once a month for dinner and celebrated holidays together as families. Though our family moved away physically, something in me remained with these friends over the miles.

I wondered, even felt some sense of guilt, that they were willing to expend so much to be with us in Illinois. They never knew how much we needed them; neither did we until they arrived and finally left.

A popular song, performed by a group of outstanding recording artists for the purpose of raising funds for AIDS victims and research, is entitled "That's What Friends Are For." The lyrics are simple, the tune catchy and singable. The words are reminders of the meaning of friendship and the nature and quality of that special relationship through good times and bad times. That's what friends are for.

We all need friends, not just acquaintances. A colleague and former schoolmate more than twenty-five years ago taught me the difference. In our theological school community he was known as a no-nonsense person. He kept most people at arm's length, and he would never let others use the term *friend* lightly in reference to him or them. He would say in stern fashion, "We are acquaintances, not friends." While most often these words had a racial context, all became more cognizant of the specialness of being a friend.

We live in such an individual-oriented society that the ethos of self-sufficiency is imbedded deeply in our national psyche. Few of us escape. We admit weaknesses with difficulty; we dare not be vulnerable. We must be all-sufficient, all-knowing. Many times I have remained hopelessly lost in a city or community because I refused to ask someone for directions. What is it in me that prevented me from asking for directions? Why do I need to feel so sufficient? Why do you?

At times life becomes overwhelming for everyone. Something drives us, preventing us from acknowledging we need help or someone to talk to, someone to listen, someone to be concerned. Everyone ought to have a special someone, a person with whom he or she can laugh and cry, share fears and doubts, joys and sorrows, that special someone who knows, understands—and loves us anyway.

As my friends prepared to leave to return to their homes, we formed a fellowship circle. We joined hands, prayed, embraced, kissed, cried, and wished one another well.

"That's what friends are for," says the song, reaching out, touching, caring.

Christian trait of courtesy

It takes so little effort to be courteous. One does not have to possess great wealth, intellect, or other extraordinary characteristics. Courtesy requires no special physical prowess or theological insight. It seems such a simple thing to me.

Thus with constant amazement I observe how frequent, indeed commonplace, it is for people to specialize in discourteous, rude behavior. This routine way of relating to one another knows no group boundaries.

Politeness and courtesy are a sign of weakness to many. They go out of their way to be discourteous and want others to know that they intend to be inconsiderate.

"Good morning," "thank you," "please," a kind gesture (for fear of being labeled some kind of Neanderthal sexist, dare I give as an example a male offering a female a seat on a crowded bus or train?), seem to be signs of relationships to be avoided.

A part of my nurturing (and I suppose yours also) was the expectation that I would be polite, courteous, and under every circumstance, respectful of adults. I was taught to say "Yes, ma'am" and "Yes, sir," and the lesson was so ingrained in my psyche that I still use these titles of respect. One could be polite, I was taught, no matter what one's circumstance. It was a good lesson—not always practiced but never forgotten.

I especially remember a period during the turbulent 1960s, that rebellious time, when cherished and long-held values were challenged and smashed. It became chic in many circles to shock, to be profane, to avoid any gesture of respect or politeness. People went out of their way to hurt one another. Thank God that era has passed!

An absence of courtesy toward one another still exists. Too

frequently the expectation is that relationships can function without it. I remember how shocked I was to enter a theological school community and discover that both faculty and students passed one another in hallways without so much as a "Good morning." Today this happens typically among persons who relate to one another but share common tasks. It is strange!

How many times persons sit side by side at worship and never speak to one another. They sing and pray about fellowship and concern for brothers and sisters but ignore the one seated next to them. Some of my most lonely moments have been in worship. To ignore others in church seems the height of insensitivity and incongruity.

At a time when so much estrangement, loneliness, and uncertainty exist in society, politeness and courtesy to one another carry far more important meanings than many may expect. Many mornings when I have been preoccupied, anxious, or just down, a smile, a "Good morning" or "Hi" has made a difference. Or perhaps someone opened a door for me, or I for that person, and we each sensed a moment of mutual affirmation.

We often turn to the *big* issues when assessing what makes life meaningful. I am discovering that if we were to practice the art of perfecting the little, simple acts of daily living in relationships, life would be a more pleasant experience.

To be courteous is defined in one place as "marked by respect for and consideration of others." Those are a part of Christian character.

Emerson once said, "Life is not so short but that there is always time enough for courtesy."

Certainly everybody—no one excluded—can be courteous!

Words can create blessing or pain

Words are important. I like to organize, dissect, listen to, and even create them. They are more than vehicles of communication; they can be mind expanding, pushing me beyond the pedestrian to some yet undiscovered world. Words ought to be protected, nourished, and used with care. They are powerful.

As a boy, I learned a little rhyme popular at that time: "Sticks and stones may break my bones, but names will never harm me."

How I recall reciting those words to companions who had just devastated me by discovering the right name to damage my little ego. Even as I denied it, the pain was severe. I knew in my little boy way if words could not harm, they could hurt me. The residue of that hurt scarred my ego and soul years later. The reality is that words can both hurt and heal. So often they hurt without one knowing or intending such. An expression typically used with one connotation in a particular setting becomes an offense and an insult in another.

I shall never forget attending a Christmas party at the home of a parishioner. We were quite close. She was supportive and understanding, even protective of her fresh-out-of-seminary pastor. It was a joyous affair, characteristic of such festivities during the Christmas season. After dinner, as we sat in the living room munching on a variety of goodies, my host politely lifted a dish of nuts from the table and said, "Have some of these nigger toes!" Without pause she continued her conversation. She meant no harm. Indeed, she never gave a thought to what she had said.

As a general secretary of a United Methodist general agency some years ago, I prepared a questionnaire to secure statistics on the composition of the denomination's constituency. The form contained three identification categories—white, black, other. What is an *other*? I had offended without intending to do so. Do you remember when it was acceptable to refer to persons as "dumb," "a dame," or "crippled"? When used, none of these words intended to hurt or insult, but we have since discovered they did and still do.

On other occasions words damage people when they are chosen intentionally to hurt or to insult another person. Sometimes there is an effort to disguise, but only slightly so that the object of the insult does not miss the intent. Frequently, married people know exactly the words to use to bring pain, even tears, to a mate. Colleagues and friends know how to get under one's skin.

It is important that we take more seriously our use of words. When we feel alone, we hear words that break through the loneliness and give us a sense of belonging or acceptance—a simple word, such as *friend*.

When there has been a breach in a relationship with possibly no way to reconcile differences, words such as "I am sorry," or "forgive me," or "I didn't intend it to come out that way," are healing words. Words that embrace and include the whole human family so that no one feels left out or less important because of gender, status, or racial identity are words that heal. Elie Wiesel, Nobel Peace Prize recipient, has said, "Words can sometimes, in moments of grace, attain the quality of deeds."

Yet neither should words imprison. Howard Thurman, author and preacher, used to say something like this: "I want to be me without making it difficult for you to be you!" We must not become chauvinistic about words. What I desire may be an unfair imposition on another's right to be who he or she needs to be.

The first and only time my father overheard me using profanity, he quickly whacked me across the face (he was no pacifist!) and forced me to repeat, "Profanity is the effort of the weak mind to express itself forcefully!"

At times, indeed, we must express our thoughts and positions forcefully. Yet it is important that the words we choose be as noble as the cause we espouse. Sometimes ill-chosen words for a worthy effort have resulted in the failure of the listener to hear, not because the cause was not worthwhile, but because the words distracted the listener from its truth.

Beth Day, in a poem entitled "Three Gates of Gold," says that before you speak, you should ask three questions: "Is it true? Is it needful? Is it kind?"

Miracles of Dependence

I believe the ministry of healing is a gift to the church. It cannot be learned in school or seminar; it cannot be passed on from one generation to another. It can only be discovered by the one who has been blessed by the gift. There are indeed those times when the gift is found in a community of believers.

When angels rejoice

I've known him for twenty-five years. He is an effective and able clergyman. As a seminarian he was challenging, some might even say angry. His ministry has been devoted almost entirely as a local church pastor. An activist, my friend has conscientiously and intentionally endeavored to apply the gospel to his social setting. In my judgment he has been a faithful servant.

Recently I attended a workshop on spiritual formation led by my old colleague. Like most of us after twenty-five years, he has mellowed. Yet he is just as intense. He recounted his faith journey for the participants. I was surprised at his candor, but I shouldn't have been. He insightfully shared his spiritual peaks and valleys. Then he recounted a moving incident.

He said that several years ago he had become drained. The years of activism and ministry had taken their toll. "I was just burned out. I had nothing more to give." Recognizing his physical, emotional, and spiritual fatigue, he went to God empty and exhausted. He prayed a simple but fervent prayer, "Lord I can't do any more! I'm tired, I just can't do any more."

My friend said, "I believe I heard the angels rejoicing, 'Praise God, he can't do any more! He can't do any more!'"

New life begins for many persons when they reach their limit and can go no longer or no further on their own ingenuity, talents, or strength. Their own faith is insufficient.

This may come particularly to those who are self-assured. Successful, effective, and gifted, they seem to take life in stride. For them God seems more a convenience than a need. They take God for granted.

We tend to look at the valleys in life as points of defeat. Sometimes we are embarrassed by our failure and inadequacy.

"Why, I've never had a problem I couldn't handle," we reason. "I've been able to bounce back from every setback I've ever faced," some say in puzzlement.

Even physical limitations surprise us. "I've never missed a meeting or a day at work." "Sermons always came so easily." "The first two children were never a problem!" "I was always so healthy." The litany of surprise goes on. We reach our wit's end. We can do absolutely nothing else.

My friend is right. I believe the angels do rejoice, "Praise God, she can't do any more! He can't do any more!" These moments of apparent devastation, instead of being life-threatening, can in fact be life-altering—life-changing. Sometimes we must be taken to our knees before we can stand tall again. The reminders come in various ways, often painfully, that even our best at times is insufficient. None of us is an inexhaustible machine that simply rolls on and on.

Spiritual giants, those whose spiritual depth others admire and seek to emulate, have their moments of self-awareness, the realization of their limitations. My friend says he had a new birth. He called it a new conversion. I can attest to the truth of his witness.

Maybe when you find yourself at the place in your faith journey that you are exhausted and burned out, and have no answers, little strength, or a sense of hopelessness, the angels will sing that paradoxical song for you—"Praise God, she can't do any more!" "Praise God, he can't do any more!"

Then you can observe a mighty God at work.

A hostile or trusting heart

It has long been argued that there is an inextricable relationship of mind and body. The debate centers on the exact nature of that relationship and the degree to which the observation is true.

A newspaper article dealing with this subject captured my interest and attention. It explored the effect of emotions on wellness. Recalling a study done some thirty years ago, the writer of the article discussed the impact of personality traits on serious illness. The study divided individuals into two basic personality types—Type A and Type B. "Type A behavior: In a hurry, impatient, often angry. Type B behavior: Laid back, calm, slow to anger, good listeners."

The doctors involved in the study concluded, "Type A's more often fell victim to heart attacks: Type B's less so."

One doctor looking at this data has said, "We have strong evidence now that hostility . . . damages the heart." The impact of anger on blood pressure, he suggests, can be debilitating and even fatal.

The article points out: "To be hostile means that you want to hurt or punish somebody. . . . To have 'free floating hostility' means that you are angry, or on the point of anger, much of the time, with or without major cause."

I'll have to let the medical community debate the validity of the part hostility plays in some heart attacks, but I do know something about hostility. I encounter it more frequently than I would like to admit. It seems to be increasing in our society. One stereotypically thinks of childhood as a happy time of life. Yet even children express an alarmingly high incidence of hostility and intense anger.

Hostility is not limited by socioeconomic status, race, gender, or profession. I know and have met hostile people fitting every description. Something in them has somehow gotten twisted. Perhaps at one time there was a cause for the anger, but the hostility has become all-consuming and takes on a life of its own. It is anger for anger's sake!

Some persons remain hostile despite circumstances. This distinguishes justifiable from destructive anger. The resolution of conflict and reconciliation of persons do not affect or change the anger. Hostility seems permanent rather than temporary.

I don't know whether or not such an attitude contributes to heart attacks. I'm sure the argument has advocates on both sides of the issue. What I do believe is that constant hostility makes for unhappy living. Frowns rather than smiles, criticism rather than compliment, and cynicism instead of trust certainly have their peculiar pain.

Dr. Redford Williams, a psychiatrist at Duke University

studying the relationship of hostility and anger to health, has written a book entitled *How to Have a Trusting Heart.* He holds that hostility is related to mistrust of others. He offers a list of suggestions for reducing hostility and becoming a more trusting person. Among these is "Confess your hostility. . . . And practice forgiveness."

Confession and forgiveness are familiar concepts to us in the Christian community. They mark central points of our doctrine and faith.

We need times of introspection; times of confession and forgiveness; times to examine our lives, thoughts, and actions. Long before the advent of modern medicine and psychiatry the psalmist implored, "Search me, O God and know my heart, test me and know my thoughts. See if there is any wicked way in me, and lead me in the way everlasting" (Psalm 139:23-24 NRSV).

Here is a good beginning.

Speaking of (in) adequacy!

I don't know if a sense of inadequacy sometimes touches all of us; it seems to visit me often. Just facing life and the demands of tasks cries out for our best, and in our heart of hearts we know better than others that our best is inadequate.

Many persons possess a strong sense of self, a healthy awareness of their abilities in what they can accomplish and withstand. I have long admired them. They seem to have it all together—a kind of wholeness of life. The inner and outer selves seem to be at one. They stand like the strong oak withstanding storms and torrents of pain, despair, conflict, and sorrow. They seem utterly adequate. We can learn from them.

Then there are the rest of us. Those whose sense of inadequacy seems ever present are found in many walks of life, holding a variety of titles and perhaps impressive credentials.

Sometimes inadequacy comes from a long history of low self-esteem. Not always aware of when and how it happened, one day you simply realize that your sense of self lacks strength and stability. Others always seem better, stronger, and more able. Struggle as you will, there never emerges that certain sense of self that brings stability and certainty. The struggle continues.

Some struggle with the sense of inadequacy when the presence of their ability, personableness, and skill is obvious to others. Yet those who struggle lack a sense of assurance.

It is strange how the interaction of these qualities fails to synthesize into a sense of wholeness. To have it all and yet not have it all together is especially frustrating and bewildering. Loved ones and colleagues stand in wonderment as they watch one so endowed struggle to find a sense of adequacy. It seems so apparent.

Feelings of inadequacy, in another sense, are healthy and normal if for no other reason than that we *are* inadequate. Who is adequate for all tasks, demands, and life's surprises and devastations? A sense of adequacy in all things may be, after all, an illusion—a contradiction of creation itself.

A growing individualism and a failure to feel the need of community may be the frightening results of a prosperous, materialistic age in which the goal is the attainment of adequacy and self-reliance in all things.

Maybe a healthy sense of inadequacy is a built-in reminder that we are strengthened in and by community. I am discovering that the three hardest words for many to say are "I don't know." The single most difficult word to say is "Help!" This, after all, is what community is all about. It is to respond to help, to answer "I don't know."

One of the main purposes of creation was to forge community. God knew and knows that a sense of inadequacy is a part of the human condition and human nature itself. But it is one in which inadequacy becomes not pathos but gift. It is not a state but a phase when inadequacy is made adequate by others and by God. Some inadequacies belong to God, and God alone can make the wounded whole.

Other inadequacies don't deserve God's time, for God has already provided the inner resources to make one adequate. Some are opportunities given to the community to remind it that its strength is in its connectedness—the strong to the weak, the inadequate to the adequate. Or a sense of inadequacy may be one of those God opportunities that we frequently overlook!

Gift of healing is authentic

When she anointed me with oil, I was rather surprised. I was able to maintain my composure and could sense at once I was not alone in my discomfort.

On another occasion when the service in which I was participating ended, the announcement was made there would follow a service of healing and anointing. I remained for that service not so much to participate as to observe.

The healing ministry of the church has not had great emphasis, especially in United Methodism. In my early ministry, I was highly suspicious of those claiming the power to perform physical healing. As a boy I was exposed to a variety of "faith healing" experiences. Most proved to be less than authentic. Stories of exploitation of persons suffering from serious illness, often fatal, have been heard and told by many with firsthand experiences.

To be sure, the gift of healing is scriptural. Jesus healed, as did the disciples and apostles. It is a valid ministry of the church, but one to be undertaken with the greatest of care, sensitivity, and scrutiny.

The healing ministry of the church should not be limited to physical healing. There is need for emotional and spiritual as well as relational healing. Healing must be holistic.

While I still look with a jaundiced eye on those claiming the gift of physical healing, my belief in the efficacy of healing is not shaken. Such belief is grounded in an omnipotent God and not the sometimes too easy claims of "faith healers," especially those who require handsome financial contributions for the performance of their "gift."

I do believe in miracles—the occurrence of acts not explained by rational and logical reasoning, cures and healings that have taken place in the face of contrary medical prediction and evidence. The laying on of hands and prayers for the sick, broken, and emotionally anguished, resulting in wholeness and healing, has occurred sufficiently that miracles exist in the realm of possibility. This is more testimony to the power of God than the claims of men and women.

If one could explain such miracles, then they would no longer be miracles. If they occurred routinely, they would lose their miraculous character. The fact that such physical healing occurs so unpredictably makes the charge of a capricious God seem all too possible.

I believe the ministry of healing is a gift to the church. It cannot be learned in school or seminar; it cannot be passed on from one generation to another; it can only be discovered by the one who has been blessed by the gift. There are indeed those times when the gift is found in a community of believers.

The Christian community must always be sensitive to those who would exploit and use those of God's people who so desperately look for hope and healing as to make them vulnerable to charlatans and false prophets. For they are everywhere, prepared to take advantage of those who are weak and who long for that cure, healing, and wholeness.

A friend, a prominent and nationally known social activist, shocked me some years ago when I learned that he held weekly services of healing in his local church. He seemed so unlikely, so uncharacteristic of what I imagined as one who would participate in the ministry of healing. Yet he had seen and been a part of God's healing in the lives of countless people.

Someone has said the question she most desired God to answer was "Why were some people healed and others not?" What a question! I, too, long for the answer. But until I get it, I will continue to marvel at God's miracles, encourage the church to engage in the ministry of healing—physical, emotional, spiritual, relational—and expose those frauds within and outside the church who seem to make a mockery of one of God's most amazing gifts to the church—the gift of healing.

The hush of silence nurtures body and mind

Silence is an increasingly precious and rare gift. Our society is bombarded by near perpetual sound and noise. It would seem that we are afraid of silence. I used to be!

Growing up in the city, I was constantly surrounded by its sounds—voices, automobiles, radios, televisions, music. Sound was my friend. Noises were welcomed; silence was not.

Modern technology has made possible the avoidance of silence except when sleeping. An increasing number of people leave television and radio on even in sleeping hours.

We can carry music with us wherever we go. People jog with earphones, young people carry large, awkward, blaring radios— the larger and louder presumably providing more status. Elevator hallways, office buildings, and doctors' offices are filled with music or talk shows. Even the farm now has lost its solace, and the sounds of farm machinery fill the day.

When groups of people gather in the office or around the dinner table or for coffee, note how awkward are the moments of silence. Even when there is nothing more to be said, people feel compelled to talk.

It is difficult to find a time of silence in worship. Moments of silent prayer are helped along with appropriate background music and dare not go too long for fear the worshipers will become bored or impatiently conclude time is being wasted.

We are a people drowned in sound. It is not that sounds of life are bad for us. On the contrary, they bring a certain buoyancy; they are a kind of music to our ears. As we need a time for symphony of sound, we likewise need the melody of silence.

Utter silence, with only you and silence and God, is a time to reflect and listen to what silence has to say. It gives the ears reprieve, the voice a time to rest, body and mind the chance to slow down and be refilled and renewed.

Some have to go away to a silent place if they are fortunate to have such a place. Others might find it, of all places, at home when everyone is gone and at last one can be alone and embrace the gift of silence. Some, knowing that the moments of authentic silence are so rare that they will have to endure for a spell, gobble them frantically.

Now I welcome silence. Perhaps as one grows older there is a greater appreciation for it. It may well be that the senses can no longer absorb the constant traffic of sound. Or there might just be the greater need for silence.

Perhaps the soul and mind go too long without the nurture of silence. I fear we pay a heavy price for our constant activity, incessant speaking, and sound-filled days and nights.

"Be still and know that I am God." The stillness of silence allows us to encounter self and God in a unique way. Perhaps then and only then God gets our undivided attention.

Lent mirrors imperfections

During the season of Lent the wish to be perfect becomes more pronounced. To have what one wills and what one does always conform is a longed-for desire. Sometimes I think bishops should be perfect; it ought to come with the consecration service! During the ceremony when the bishops of the church lay hands on the head of the newly elected bishop, that should be the moment when all blemishes and imperfections miraculously disappear.

Bishops then could become all that is expected of them: long-suffering, courageous, free of pride and prejudices, always forgiving, and the paradigm of spiritual virtue. They ought to be endowed with unquestioned wisdom, unlimited patience, and, of course, boundless energy. Especially should they be beyond temptations and unkind or unwholesome thoughts. And they should know how to think through every issue to avoid saying the wrong thing or making a bad decision.

Never are my imperfections more glaring than during the season of Lent. For me it is a time of intense personal scrutiny. Daily I spiritually undress before God, free of title and ecclesiastical garb; I stand, wait, and confess. The painfully embarrassing encounter always overflows with too much to confess. My life is never as exemplary as I would wish, my faith not nearly as strong or secure. Sometimes the harder I try the more I miss the mark.

The spiritual mirror is unflatteringly honest. It never reflects what we think we are, or how we would like to appear to others. The cosmetics that cover some blemish, some imperfection, seem utterly invisible to the spiritual reflection. However, the stark reality of how we really look without all the cosmetic aids to make us polished, sparkling, and fresh is similar to the way we look when rising from a night's sleep before brushing our teeth, showering, shaving, grooming our hair, or applying makeup.

God might have made it easier to obtain the level of spiritual maturity and exemplary life desired or willed. To will it should be to achieve it. Titles and status ought to assure it. Such certainly should come with education, economic security, and age. Even belonging to the "right" denomination ought to help.

So I undress before God and I stand before the mirror of eternity. In my naked imperfections I discover a mercy I did not expect or deserve. For the reflection is not only that of what I am, but of what I can become. Each imperfection is coupled with the image of what I am expected to be. Each misdeed is accompanied by the good deed offered. How I appear is not the sum total of all I am, but rather what I can become in Christ.

In the quiet of each day I stand and encounter self and God, always disappointed in what is revealed and how and where I have failed. I am surprised often at the times and places, indeed the frequency of my failings. One by one I recall and recite them—names of persons wronged, acts committed, thoughts thought, deeds left undone. So many, so many. The soul weeps even as God weeps with me and for me.

The encounter with God always ends the same way—the words come with such clarity, judgment, and compassion— "Your sins are forgiven; go, therefore, and sin no more." So I try once again.

Returns of Evil for Evil

Everywhere I turn I see brokenness, a sense of meaningless-ness among all classes and races. Disturbing statistics, the morning paper, and the evening news dramatically illustrate a sense of lostness. We see it in our community, sometimes in our own family. It often seems to me a struggle the Church is losing.

I grieve when I witness how easily today's advocates of tolerance become tomorrow's disciples of intolerance, how groups and individuals in their quest for equal rights become insensitive to the rights of others. How quickly and easily the oppressed can become the oppressor.

The church versus itself

Now it's the abortion issue. Only a few years ago it was busing. Both seem to have generated the same kind of emotional intensity. At one time it was war versus pacifism.

Christians always find something about which to fight each other.

The Church has expended so much of its resources, energy, and time battling itself, it's no wonder that it is losing influence in the larger community and has diminishing impact on shaping moral and ethical behavior.

Some of the most hostile confrontations I've witnessed have been those not of believer against non-believer, but between believers. Fundamentalists attack conservatives, conservatives attack liberals, and vice versa. Charismatics question the authenticity of belief of those who manifest the Spirit in different gifts.

I imagine Satan, or however you name the power of evil, enjoys the constant quarrelling and fighting among religious people. It has been going on for thousands of years, so it may be naive to think that it would not be prevalent today.

The list goes on: God's nature and character, the meaning and number of sacraments, the authenticity of miracles. The religious community has agreed to disagree on many of these important fundamental tenets.

Frequently I receive a letter from a United Methodist demanding to know what the bishop believes about this or that. Underlying most of these inquiries may be the writer's assumption that my view on one tenet or social issue cancels out my belief on all others. It is one-issue theology similar to one-issue politics.

Abortion is for many that kind of pivotal concern upon which one's Christianity is validated or questioned. For others the issue is sexism, racism, or the place and accuracy of scriptures.

Each religious group or denomination, of course, determines the degree of orthodoxy required of its adherents. Each decides areas of flexibility and levels of differing opinion that a follower is allowed in order to remain in good standing. This is the right and role of organized religion.

What is troubling and difficult is the animosity generated within the Church and often within a denomination. Something little less than hatred best describes attitudes held by some Christians against others. They call one another names or paint others with less than precise labels—all in the name of Christ.

Everywhere I turn I see brokenness, a sense of meaninglessness among all classes and races. Disturbing statistics, the morning paper, and the evening news dramatically illustrate a sense of lostness. We see it in our community, sometimes in our own family. It often seems to me a struggle the Church is losing.

Cannot the Christian community, although broad in its perspective—conservative to liberal to orthodox—adjust itself to a common agenda to meet such needs?

I am weary of so much time, energy, and money being used by Christians in general and some United Methodists in particular in fighting each other, while the number of unchurched and unsaved continues to grow, while broken lives remain in pieces and the lost continue in estrangement. Wouldn't it be a pity if the world God loves so much were ignored because the Church was too busy doing battle with itself?

No longer silent

I don't know when this blatant disregard and disrespect for women began manifesting itself in physical abuse. How long has it been with us? Are we made more conscious today because of dramatic cases appearing in the media, or the seemingly increasing number of reported incidents by women?

How long has society sent mixed signals about the worth and

value of women? Or about their "place"? On the one hand, our culture views women as special, needing preferred treatment and special protection by society in general and men in particular. Customs, traditions, and eventually laws have been enacted to give legal status to preferred treatment.

On the other hand, a different view has been fostered both subtly and not so subtly. I don't recall when I first saw the cartoon of the cave man with club in one hand and the hair of a woman in the other as she was dragged along the ground in helplessness. We all saw it. Some laughed, others smiled, but the caricature carried a message about male-female relationships and a view of women that influenced men and women alike.

Today's statistics are staggering. In a day when it is believed under-reporting of physical abuse of women still goes on, the number abused each year grows by the thousands. Fortunately more women have decided to suffer in silence no longer. They come out of the closet after having endured years of abuse.

Unfortunately others endure abuse in silence. Some feel trapped, holding on to the "security" of family. Others fear for their lives and the lives of their children. Some can't bear the embarrassment that such revelation would bring to what appears to be a typical happy marriage or family.

One of my greatest concerns is the role society plays in forming attitudes and influencing behaviors that manifest themselves in physical abuse of women.

In some communities both young men and women soon accept abusive behavior as a part of normal male-female relationships. Young men report their first physical abuse of a girlfriend as a mark of male maturity. And sadly, many teenage girls report the first slap received from a boyfriend with a strange sense of pride. Perhaps such showed they were "really loved."

Somewhere, sometime, a message is sent that it's okay for women to be manhandled under certain circumstances. Some youngsters have gotten the message as early as their elementary years.

Physical abuse of women occurs among all groups—racial,

ethnic, and socioeconomic. It is a rural and an urban problem and occurs among the old and the young.

While churches and religious organizations have addressed sexual violence, as rightfully they should, the incidence of physical violence endured by women in the privacy of their homes is by far a greater problem. It has too long been ignored.

While the causes of physical abuse of women by men are many, the behavior pattern can no longer be ignored, tolerated, excused, or rationalized. Under no circumstances can it be condoned!

Supporting shelters for battered women and children is a need the churches and government can address all across the nation, but that alone is not enough. Indeed in some ways that response is too late.

The greater need is to determine what we can do and say, what we model and promote, that will enhance respect for women. These attitudes might ensure that physical harm would not even be contemplated by men, let alone exercised. Institutionally our media must be held more accountable as well.

As one resolution adopted by the United Methodist General Conference declares: "As Christians, we need to examine those materials with which we interact to determine their social or physical violence characteristics. We must ensure that we do not communicate myths that perpetuate violence or allow images of violence, victimization, or exploitation to become a part of institutional communications."

The physical abuse of women has been tolerated too long. Enough is enough!

Sexual harassment

It's called sexual harassment. While the term is of recent coinage, the act is not. It is and has been experienced by women (primarily but not exclusively) for too long. For the most part they have silently endured the humiliation and violation of their persons and bodies. But that day is past! Or at least it is passing.

Slowly and somewhat timidly at first women began speaking out against the verbal, mental, and physical abuse they have undergone in the workplace. Society is now being made aware and aroused by the many reports from women of all backgrounds on what they have experienced in their place of employment.

The problem is of such proportions that such acts are now defined as violations of one's civil rights. Title 29, Code of Federal Regulations, subsection 1604.11, provides:

> Sexual harassment—(a. harassment on the basis of sex is a violation of Sec. 703 of Title VII (the Civil Rights Act of 1964). Unwelcome sexual advances, requests for sexual favors, and other verbal or physical conduct of a sexual nature constitute sexual harassment when 1) Submission to such conduct is made either explicitly or implicitly a term or condition of individual employment, 2) Submission to or rejection of such conduct by an individual is used as a basis for employment decisions affecting such individual or, 3) Such conduct has the purpose or effect of unreasonably interfering with an individual's work performance or creating an intimidating, hostile, or offensive work environment.)

No woman or man (the legislation is gender neutral) should have to suffer the insult of unwanted and imposed and otherwise demeaning overtures from employer or colleague. To be the target of such behavior is to make one an *It* (an object) rather than a *Thou*. We stand solidly in our Christian tradition that holds that persons are *Thous*, ends in themselves, and not *Its*, means to an end.

Sexual harassment in all forms treats persons as sex objects. They are seen as a means to an end—the sexual satisfaction and gratification of the harasser. The Christian, and indeed the Church, should always say no to such actions whether they are actions of a person, a nation, or society itself.

Women, for they have been the primary ones abused, are entering the work force in record numbers. The number of female-headed households increases monthly. The great percentage of working women is in the workplace not only because women want to be but because they must be. The two-member wage earning family is becoming the norm and not the exception.

Regrettably, too many women endure the harassment silently, reasoning "that's just the way it is." If that's the way it is, that's not the way it ought to be. To give an honest day's work for a decent and just wage is what is required—nothing more and nothing less.

Persons should have a sense of satisfaction in their work and not be made to feel less than full persons in the process. The workplace should be one in which the atmosphere is conducive to productive and efficient performance. Both employer and employees have responsibilities to see that such is the case.

The legislation against sexual harassment further evidences an enlightened view when it states:

(f. Prevention is the best tool for the limitation of sexual harassment. An employer should take all steps necessary to prevent sexual harassment from occurring, such as affirmatively raising the subject, expressing strong disapproval, developing appropriate sanctions, informing employees of their right to raise and how to raise the issue of harassment under Title VII, and developing methods to sensitize all concerned.

Whether one is employer or employee, clergy or laity, man or woman, the highest standard of behavior is expected. To treat another as an object, sexual or otherwise, is always wrong.

Sexual harassment should not, cannot, and will not be tolerated any longer in any organization either outside or inside the Church. For the Church it is not just the issue of a civil right but more profoundly a theological wrong!

War costs more than we can pay

It was a poignant moment, moving and sad. My mind flashed back to another time and place. . . .

I didn't want them to go to Vietnam. In fact I protested and demonstrated to express my opposition to the war. But many went anyway! Some went out of a sense of patriotism and duty, others because it afforded a degree of security (how ironic!), others because they could not dare think of not going.

I sat on the platform with distinguished military personnel, politicians, and civic leaders. I was to give the benediction at the dedication of the Illinois Vietnam Veterans Memorial.

I have visited the Vietnam Memorial in Washington many times, early in the morning, late at night, in summer and in winter. Always it is heart-wrenching. The names of the dead, like the crosses at Arlington Cemetery, seem endless. I look for no name in particular; I read each one and that only increases the pain.

I didn't want them to go, although I think I understand their going. But I still don't like war—that one or any other.

The Illinois Vietnam Veteran's Memorial is located in Oak Ridge Cemetery in Springfield. The walls, like the one in Washington, are made of black granite, but they are circular in design.

The names of the dead are engraved and stand out against the black granite. Five inner walls made of gray granite contain the names of those missing in action.

Nearly three thousand names appear on the black and gray granite walls, all Illinoisans. Here they hold a common destiny, however different they may have been in life.

Seated in the bright, hot sun that Saturday afternoon, I pondered. War . . . I wish nations would be as dedicated to peace as they seem to be to war.

I looked out on the faces of family members and friends who had gathered to remember, pay tribute, and weep. They were sons and daughters, fathers and mothers, wives now widows, and sweethearts. I had not seen so many men weep—strong, now not as young. Some were in wheelchairs.

War is so obsolete, yet we seem not to want to give it up. We've grown so accustomed to it; some nations can't recall a time when they were not at war.

We teach our young about war and condition them when they are most impressionable. We introduce them to war games, give them toys of war, and when they become adults they believe in the inevitability of war.

Lands are covered with the remains of the war dead and our dreams and broken hearts. Sometimes freedom is the result of war, but not always. But war is not what I thought of that day; it was the children of war, for they were so young—or so most soldiers seem. They were in the prime of life.

Paradoxically, I have never been against soldiers, only against war! Soldiers are only sons and daughters in uniform. Without their uniforms, they have no distinguishing characteristics. They laugh and love, dream and hope. Life to them is as precious as are they—precious creatures of a loving God, given to earth for life and fulfillment.

I thought of them that day, especially those who died and those still reported missing in that strange war of Vietnam. They are honored, remembered, and missed. Their names now stand as a constant reminder for all to see.

I will visit the monument again in a more leisurely and quiet fashion, and then I will talk to the names.

I hope we will always remember the high cost of war—not the huge military budgets or the costly, sophisticated weaponry, but the human cost: our young and not so young, those who love life yet risk and give theirs, families who will never be quite the same because of the loss and absence of a loved one.

It is not just soldiers who die in wars but our neighbors, our friends, our relatives—precious human beings, God's children. What a price! War is expensive—as is freedom.

My prayer given on that day seemed pale in the light of what they had given. I offered words; they offered their lives.

I pledged once more never to take freedom for granted, to do nothing to mar or deny it to others, but to embrace, strengthen, and preserve it.

And I prayed for a day when nations would study war no more.

The Holocaust remembered: "Never again" has a hollow ring

The old state capitol in Springfield, now the Hall of Representatives, was darkened with shades drawn to keep out the bright sunlight of the warm spring day. People greeted one another with obvious familiarity, but once in the hall there was only somberness. Men received yarmulkes as they entered.

It was a somber occasion. It is called "Days of Remembrance," Yom ha-Sho'ah. This Holocaust commemoration is held annually as Jews around the world gather to remember the six million men, women, and children who perished during the most despicable crime against humanity yet recorded. Gentiles join them, too, and remember.

As speaker after speaker remembered, some with voices breaking, their most repeated words were "Never again!" Never again will the populace remain silent while a people are systematically tortured, brutalized, or slaughtered. Never again!

That was a sad period of world history. As the only Protestant clergyperson participating, I felt the weight of the indictment against the Church, which for the most part ignored what was taking place against members of the human family. There was an overwhelming sense of guilt. As each speaker remembered the silence and inaction of religious as well as political leaders, I cringed. The sins of the fathers and mothers now fell upon this son. Something inside of me began a steady, rhythmic chant, "Never again—never again!"

Representatives from across the state were a part of this statewide observance—rabbis, mayors, civic and political leaders, including the governor. Young and old were present, as were some relatives of those who perished in the Holocaust. But the most moving moment occurred during a candle lighting ceremony led by a local rabbi. One by one the unlit candles that had been on a stand in front of the hall were lit as the people remembered acts of discrimination, oppression, heinous biological experimentation, torture, and death. It was difficult to hold back the tears; some didn't try.

As we vowed never to let such atrocities scorch this earth again, my mind began to race. I saw pictures, recalled news accounts, and began to doubt. I believe it could, does, and will happen again. I pray to God that it not happen in the proportions of World War II; never could we allow six million human beings to be destroyed again. But is the number the crucial factor? How much brutality are we willing to tolerate—sixty, six hundred, six thousand?

Today governments do ostracize, brutalize, imprison, and execute. Men, women, and children are systemically disenfranchised, mutilated, starved, and destroyed. The tolerance level of the general populace, world leaders, and even the Church is appallingly high.

There seems to be a stratification of life. Not all human life is of equal value. A person's importance as a human being still is linked with external factors—political ideology or party, race or religion, gender or economic status. People become aroused about the inhumane treatment of others only if those being mistreated are members of a particular category of the human family. How sad.

As long as this is our assessment of the human family, and the manner in which we measure the worth of human beings, I see no reason to believe or expect that a holocaust can't happen again. I hope I'm wrong.

Oppressed and oppressor have common flaws

A haunting phrase will not leave my mind: Today's oppressed can be tomorrow's oppressor! It is not a prophecy, but a reminder of the character flaw that seems to evidence itself continually in individuals and nations. Those who know the full weight of oppression, prejudice, and intolerance are expected to be more sensitive to and demonstrative in ways of peace, love, justice, and freedom.

One would expect the victims of oppression to remember. Yet everywhere illustrations remind us of how quickly they forget. People who were once dominated by foreign powers are hardly through their victory celebration of the overthrow before they are dominated again by their own governmental leaders.

Some of the most heinous atrocities are committed by citizens against citizens. Maimings, threats, and imprisonments are increasingly not the result of some wicked foreign power, but are perpetrated by neighbor against neighbor, brother and sister against each other, governments against those who elected them to places of trust. If one has no place in one's theological framework for a concept of original sin, it certainly will cause some deep reflection and reconsideration.

Are freedom, fair play, and justice reserved only for particular groups or individuals? As nations, peoples, and any number of so-called minority groups seek to achieve justice, are the noble words toward these ends only selfishly subscribed? Are they not objective ends for the human family? Do the words and efforts have only temporary meaning until they have been achieved by a particular oppressed or subjugated people?

In the scheme of things we sometimes identify virtues and vices with predetermined categories. The definitions of heroes and villains are always oversimplified. Good is resident here and evil there. Certain political persuasions are always wrong, while others are always right. With disappointment we discover that evil is not intrinsic to any nation or group, race or political persuasion, or to either gender. The tendency toward intolerance, hatred, violence, and injustice has apparently been equally distributed.

Yet a gnawing inside me keeps saying, "You should know better!" You ought not to inflict on others the very injustices you challenged and demanded not be inflicted on you. It is in fact one of the oldest and most widespread philosophical and religious dictums: "Do unto others as you would have them do unto you." One could almost say that if every other philosophical and theological tenet were eliminated except this one, the world and its people would have achieved the highest ethical posture attainable.

I grieve when I witness how easily today's advocates of tolerance become tomorrow's disciples of intolerance, how groups and individuals in their quest for equal rights become insensitive to the rights of others. How quickly and easily the oppressed can become the oppressor!

Selfishness, greed, and thirst for power are potent realities. Their ability to seduce and consume are overwhelming. They seem to engulf the most noble of today's dreams and turn them into tomorrow's most horrific nightmares. These flaws of will and character continue to undermine our hopes and dreams for peace and justice. Always there's human need, it seems, for some to be at the top while others are at the bottom; always there must be oppressed and oppressor, victim and perpetrator.

I still expect, perhaps naively, the oppressed and those who have known the depth of intolerance to reflect a higher ethical standard.

This morning on this dark, dreary day my spirit too is dreary and my heart is heavy. And I hurt for my Palestinian brothers and sisters. I pray for them and my Israeli brothers and sisters. And I hope for a more excellent way.

Letter to Martin Luther King, Jr.

Dear Martin:

The television interviewer looked shocked, then smiled when I told him that I often write letters to those who have died. He quickly retorted, "Where do you send them?"

I could see that he immediately wished he had not responded so flippantly when he discovered I was serious. I responded, to my surprise, without pause, "I write not because the person needs to read it, but because I have a need to write it!"

So I write once more on the anniversary of your birth, Martin, not because of your need but because I need to remember, celebrate, hope. While it is becoming more difficult to do so, I know it is increasingly important that I write. I get so discouraged. I am becoming more impatient, not because I'm unappreciative of strides made in racial progress and inclusiveness. But I know as a nation we can do so much better. We have done better!

Martin, it is much like those opening lines of Charles Dickens's classic work *A Tale of Two Cities*, "It was the best of times, it was the worst of times."

Significant victories and accomplishments seem to diminish in the face of ugly prejudice and tenacious racism. The struggle to overcome both is unending. This past year especially we experienced an outbreak of violent racism and bold bigotry. It's a time of taking the bitter with the sweet, but the bitter seems so poignant. And racism, an unending labyrinth, is far more ingrained in attitude and institutional life than most perceive.

My letter, Martin, this year will be both bitter and sweet, so mingled that it is not easy to separate them. I hope you will understand.

Prejudice and racism in the North seem to get stronger daily. It is disheartening. I just read a new book by Alex Haley, *A Different Kind of Christmas*. It details the brave exploits of white abolitionists in states like Illinois, Indiana, Massachusetts, New York, and Pennsylvania. Their participation in the underground railroad made possible the freedom of countless slaves.

Their memory and deeds are today blighted by the rising bigotry in these states. It is not overstatement to observe that race relations, while a long way from ideal, are in a better state in the South than in the North.

Martin, what is most painful is to watch the young learn the practice of prejudice. I had hoped and dreamed that our young, your children and mine, might not learn firsthand the effects of prejudice that we knew. But they are learning. They experience the cruelty of the young and the insensitivity of the old. Firsthand they know racism on the campus, in the classroom and workplace, and in the church and from the pulpit. There is simply no way to protect them. I only hope we have armed them emotionally and spiritually for the inevitable.

The Church continues to be a bittersweet place. I am constantly amazed at how people of all races in the Church are able to divorce racial attitudes and behavior from Christian discipleship. Most studies still reveal that "on the average, churchgoers are more intolerant than non-churchgoers." One noted sociologist reports, "The research findings on the connection between religion and prejudice are overwhelming."

A more devastating indictment by two prominent researchers concluded: "At least for white, middle-class Christians in the United States, religion is not associated with increased love and acceptance but with increased intolerance, prejudice, and bigotry."

Martin, I don't want to believe that!

So I am proud to tell you about six white congregations here in the Central Illinois Conference who have welcomed black pastors, and as many more who are served by persons of other ethnic and racial backgrounds. Such strides go unnoticed but are cause for hope. I still believe there is a sense of decency and goodwill in the hearts of people, but racial prejudice is deeply rooted.

Maybe this year, Martin, will be marked by unparalleled progress in race relations in our land. Perhaps the church and government will once more place race as a primary agenda for their efforts and resources. Let's hope that progress, not prejudice, will make headlines.

I take courage today from your words: "Therefore, I am not yet discouraged about the future. Granted that the easygoing optimism of yesterday is impossible. Granted that we face a world crisis which leaves us standing so often amid the surging murmur of life's restless sea. But every crisis has both its dangers and its opportunities. It can spell either salvation or doom. In a dark, confused world the kingdom of God may yet reign in the hearts of [all people]."

Some thoughts on evil

Return no one evil for evil. What an ethical principle! This tenet of life is found in many religions and has a prominent place in the Christian faith. A crucified Savior's dying prayer was for those who condemned him to death.

The cross represents much to Christians; we adore it, exhibit it, wear it. It symbolizes God's love, the Savior's sacrifice, but it also represents as dramatically as anything I know this challenging ethical standard: Return no one evil for evil.

It is almost contrary to human instinct. To survive and to protect oneself are seemingly natural human responses to life. We do not have to learn them. They come with the human will: to strike back when struck, curse when cursed, hate when hated.

Some faiths sanction, indeed recognize, that such human

response is an expression of faithfulness rather than unfaithfulness. There are schools of philosophy and psychology that consider not returning evil for evil antithetical to sound mental health and normal living.

It is easier to return evil for evil. It feels right, physically and emotionally. When a blow to one's spirit, body, or character is struck, how satisfying to return in kind, or preferably with greater force and vengeance. For some it brings emotional release and a sense of wholeness. Not to do so may be interpreted as weakness or timidity and may invite continued evil deeds. So returning evil for evil becomes a way of life, a way of ordering relationships—personal and societal.

What a strange and presumably abnormal thought, this returning no one evil for evil. It smacks in the face of what it means to be fully human. Yet there it is at the heart of the gospel, at the center of the cross. One further absurdity is to love those who hate and persecute you. That simply adds insult to injury!

How inescapable it is for the Christian, how haunting and forever present for me. So often I wish it were not there. It is too constant a reminder. Jesus might have left it out of his teachings, especially if he knew how utterly impossible an ethic it is in these contemporary and complex times when evil is so evil, and when goodness seems so totally unproductive and unrewarding. Returning evil for evil seems to pay handsomely.

Yet there are those who try to make the principle of love a way of life. Not all have professed Christianity, and still they have endeavored to reflect it in manner, spirit, and deed. Mahatma Gandhi gave the ethic international prominence. Martin Luther King, Jr., used it to try to heal a nation. Mother Teresa personifies the principle and gives it human form. One who inspired me simply said, "Always be gracious to everyone, even though everyone is not always gracious to you."

But for most of us, there are no dramatic opportunities, no earth-shaking moment when human or national destiny will hang in the balance on our ethical decisions. We live out or fail to live out this challenge in more ordinary circumstances. Our context for living is with neighbor, friend, colleague, or loved one. Deeds are done, words said, and pain inflicted, all requiring some kind of response and action.

Frequently evil is done not just against our person but against our kind—our gender, status, or race. But for most it is the evil done in day-to-day ordinary relationships in the office, home, campus, and even in church. Evil is everywhere, and the perpetrators come in all colors, shapes, and garb.

There is something self-defeating about returning evil for evil, because it simply perpetuates itself into infinity. I remember the fights among my brothers and sisters. When we were separated during those childhood brawls, one of my sisters was famous for her ingenuity in being able to get in the final lick. Everybody wants to strike the last blow, but this is futile. Someone has to say, "Halt, no more!"

The doing of evil requires so much emotional and physical energy. While some may feel returning evil for evil rewarding, I just find it exhausting. Keeping score is itself a burden. Time and energy can be put to better use.

Finally, the returning of evil for evil always places others—individuals or groups—in an adversarial position. It keeps enemies as enemies and refuses to see them as brother or sister. This is contrary to the faith. Existentially it is an awful way to live.

Perhaps no teaching of Jesus is more difficult to live out on a day-to-day basis than this and its corresponding principle, love those who hate you. But keep trying!

Joys of Ordinary Gifts

Gifts that make for meaning and joy include the world's sounds, those of nature, and those born out of human creativity. For instance, there is the symphony of silence and the music of the city. Perhaps too many listen to both and hear only silence or noise. We miss the gifts. Perhaps because so many ordinary riches are bestowed upon the whole human family, they are frequently overlooked. Even those poor in material goods are rich in the countless gifts of God.

God's generous reminders

It has been some years since I've pulled a child in a sled through the snow. A recent snowfall provided me that long-forgotten joy. We bundled our grandson, Bryan Michael, in boots, gloves, muffler, hat, and hood for his first winter adventure.

Bryan moved with great effort, weighted down with the extra layers of clothing. He didn't walk so much as waddle.

Immediately attracted to his first experience of snow, he kept trying to bend over to scoop some of it into his hand. It was quite an effort.

He loved the sled ride! He giggled, laughed, and made those unintelligible sounds seventeen-month-olds make. The open soybean field seemed an endless plain for trudging and sledding. Bryan enjoyed immense freedom when we decided to walk through the snow. He could go in any direction as long as he liked without hearing those now familiar words, "no" or "stop."

When it was time to retreat to the warmth of the house he went reluctantly, crying and upset, although his cheeks and nose were red, his face and hands like ice.

Those moments were such a gift. Yet simple pleasures are too often overlooked. The accessibility of such experiences for meaning and happiness seems to be inadequately appreciated. Instead we often convince ourselves that only the acquisition and abundance of things can assure such moments. Without them we believe happiness and meaning are minimized. It is a lesson too early learned.

Surely meaning and happiness can be found in ordinary gifts of life, such as trudging in the snow with one's grandson, walking down a city street or a country road, reading and singing favorite melodies. In a high-tech, consumer-oriented society there is need to recover a proper place for such simple joys.

When persons share themselves and their ideas in conversation, joy abounds, dreams and hopes are revealed, problems are uncovered. Conversation in its own way has a healing quality. It refreshes and stimulates. What a simple, treasured gift.

Gifts that make for meaning and joy include the world's sounds, those of nature, and those born out of human creativity. For instance, there is the symphony of silence and the music of the city. Perhaps too many listen to both and hear only silence or noise. We miss the gifts. Perhaps because so many ordinary riches are bestowed upon the whole human family, they are frequently overlooked. Even those poor in material goods are rich in the countless gifts of God.

Each day I discover more of God's graciousness and generosity. My spirit is awakened to God's sensitivity to our need long before we have discovered it.

You are rich, dear ones! Such riches of life surround you. At times you may feel that God has forgotten you, perhaps even abandoned you. Who of us has not been there? You may have a deep sense of poverty—of having too little. Perhaps for that moment you have failed only to see God's reminders. Look again!

Life's best treasures may be hidden from view

Discovering the extraordinary in the ordinary is one of the secrets to successful living.

Boredom, restlessness, and even burnout come from a sense of meaninglessness. The routine exercises of daily living are approached robot-like without much thought or care. Just another day.

Viewing life in such a pedestrian fashion will undoubtedly bring one to the inevitable place—life as purposelessness.

It happens so easily and effortlessly. One can discover it only after it has taken place and without knowing when it really began. One day the realization is made that life has lost its zest, meaning, and excitement.

Sometimes that's what happens in a marriage. Two people devoted to each other, sincerely in love, and committed for life, are shocked into the realization that something radical has happened to the relationship. One or both observe that the marriage is going nowhere. It's not that there are any overwhelming problems in the relationship; it's just that there is no fulfillment in it any longer. It has become wooden, routine, and ordinary.

Place as well as relationship can take on this ordinary quality. Familiar surroundings become so familiar that they lose the quality that makes for happiness, or so it is believed. Sometimes a pastor longs to get to First Church and whatever that represents in his or her mind and understanding. That is the extraordinary place. It is understandable, a part of the human fabric, but it need not be terminal.

A member of my family is dying of cancer. He, and many others who have heard those fateful words, "You have only a year to live," have much to teach us if we would only learn. They have a perception of the extraordinary which is rooted in the ordinary. Meaning, value, and the sense of importance are found in the simple, ordinary gifts of life, those which the rest of us take for granted and often find boring or unimportant, or perhaps just ignore as having no meaning for life.

The dawning of a day: the beautiful day for most has prescribed specifications. Not so for those who understand how limited such days are for them. A day is beautiful simply in becoming. Each day becomes an extraordinary gift whether it is cloudy or sunny, cold or hot, snowy or rainy. The ordinary day becomes extraordinary.

The important things in life become less so; the not so important become more so. Laughter, friends, family, faith. Sounds and quiet. The beauty of seasons. A good book, music, and touch. The ordinary becomes extraordinary.

Relationships that are grounded in mutual caring and respect redefine love. No longer do they depend on transitory qualities such as attraction, gratification, or status. The ordinary heightens into the extraordinary.

Most of us live in the Ordinary Place. We have an ordinary family, an ordinary spouse, ordinary children, an ordinary community in which to live, an ordinary church, or an ordinary job. The great gift to ourselves is to discover how extraordinary the ordinary really is and can be.

And finally all of life is extraordinary, for it is a gift from an extraordinary God.

The church together expresses its faith

A meeting of the Council of Bishops in Arlington, Virginia, just outside Washington, D.C., provided the opportunity to return to the local church where we spent most of our years while I served with a United Methodist general agency. I was anxious to return and to worship in the congregation that meant so much to me and my family.

The fifty-mile drive through the rolling terrain of Maryland brought back so many fond memories. Familiar sights were there, horses grazing in this horse country, brand-new subdivisions alongside family farms, and beautiful, tall trees that have withstood time and changing political administrations.

My college student daughter who was accompanying me began to reminisce about the church that had nurtured her; she spoke of a church school teacher, a Christmas pageant, and choir trips. We both grew more excited as we drove into this rural region so close to the nation's capital but truly another world. We moved onto a winding road, past old farmhouses, fields being readied for planting, and cows (more cows than people were in the county when we moved there).

Then we saw the little church, a white frame building alongside the road. This had become our home church. It was part of a three-point charge. Here I had preached twice a month when the pastor preached at the other two churches. These gracious people had welcomed us and made us feel a part of the church family.

The rural and open country setting is similar to that in which many of our churches in central Illinois are found. Across the road is a wooded area (now a new subdivision is going up). Alongside the church building cows roam in a huge pasture; behind the church is the cemetery to which I had led many families in sorrow and tears.

This is what is known as a small membership church in a rural setting, and for some it is not an especially desirable place for ministry. But we chose this place more than fifteen years ago to be our church, and now I was returning. What a blessing I received!

The hugs and kisses were genuine, even a tear or two as some embraced and remembered. The little church evidenced love everywhere. The building was spotless; pews were now padded. There was no doubt of the care the congregation had for the building and for one another. We prepared for worship—what a worship service!

The robed choir processed accompanied by organ, piano, and drums. No hymn books were needed for the processional hymn. The choir and congregation sang by heart. What a marvelous phrase: "by heart." The choir and sanctuary were full. I looked about and saw all ages, from infants to those who now had to be led to their places. The worship was rich, well ordered, and the congregation sang with feeling, "Come, Holy Spirit, Come." Then the choir sang a moving contemporary arrangement of "His Eye Is on the Sparrow." There is no doubt that the Holy Spirit was present. Some joined in singing, while others clapped their hands. The inhibited simply swayed from side to side; some wept.

How my soul needed this manna, this "soul food." The sermon, preached from the weekly lectionary text, was clear, biblically grounded, full of spirit, and contemporarily relevant. As the service neared its conclusion, I knew that not only did we attend church, but "we had church!" That is a familiar phrase used in many communities across the nation. It is an affirmation that through worship there has been achieved a linking of the people and God in a real and powerful way. "We had church!"

It is not true that a rural congregation small in number with limited facilities cannot have vibrant worship and relevant ministries. Meaningful worship is not imposed on the worshipers from the outside. Rather it expresses what is on the inside, given in outward expressions in music, singing, preaching, and fellowship.

This little church on the side of the road was and still is an expression of the power of the Holy Spirit and what can happen when the faithful respond to its leading. Yes, on Sunday we had church—and on Monday we were the church.

Seeing is more than meets the eye

"Oh, I wish I could see!" she exclaimed, more in frustration than anger on a hot muggy night as we sat at an outdoor theater nestled among the trees.

We were prepared to enjoy a popular musical. We anticipated the joyful tunes, colorful costumes, and creative set designs. In spite of the heat we intended to be transported through word, dance, and song to another place. I was not prepared, however, for the drama that was to unfold in the next row.

The women sat in front of us. One was blind. She looked to be in her late teens or early twenties. The other I assumed was the mother. I unavoidably watched and listened as they chatted and waited for the production to begin. Excitement was in the air. The music began, and she said those haunting words once more, "Oh, I wish I could see!"

During the performance the young woman would turn to her mother from time to time and question, "What are they doing now? Why did they laugh? What happened then?"

The mother would lean toward her daughter and in a whisper describe the movement or look or dance. She was patient as she answered each question. Not once could I detect annoyance in her voice or demeanor; she seemed to take pride in being the eyes for another. I was moved. This seemed more important to me than what was taking place on stage.

In the middle of the production, as laughter rang out, the young woman said again more emphatically, "I wish I could see, I wish I could see!" A twinge of disgust or anger in her voice almost demanded sight! As the show went on, nonetheless she obviously was enjoying herself in spite of the momentary outburst.

So much raced through my mind that summer night: appreciation for a sensitive, patient, loving mother; admiration for a young woman deprived of sight who would not be so overwhelmed by the deprivation; encouragement from a more enlightened society that will no longer hide its less than physically perfect members.

As so often happens I look for lessons, a Word from the Lord, in even the most pedestrian events. Blindness is not an experience limited to the eyes; it can occur in the heart, mind, and spirit. So I began to think of our blindness, yours and mine. We are the sighted blind who too often do not see. We are blind to the simple beauties that surround us—the sky, the sunset, the great oak, a field plowed or ready for harvesting—splendors God has provided. We are blind to the pain of a neighbor, parishioner, friend, even a people and nation; to the feelings of others in their joy or sorrow, fear or anxiety; to loneliness; to those whose life demonstrates a thirst for "the living water"; to those who may not look, speak, or act as we do.

The young woman reminded me of an ancient admonition, "Those who have eyes, let them see." See with the eye of the heart!

Mothers are gifts of God

The day I met her at the railroad station, I was surprised because she seemed incredibly small. As we embraced and greeted each other, I had to bend more than on previous occasions to reach her. I noticed for the first time my mother was getting old.

Now, many years later, I recognize that each day of life is a gift. The body continues to go through its inevitable changes from a body of youth to one of age. Good diet, exercise, and proper medical care are evidences of good stewardship, but they can't alter this natural aging process of creation.

My mother is older now. Yet her mind is sharp, her voice strong, and her faith deep. Although her physical frame has changed dramatically and her hair is white, I still see in my mind's eye the youthful one, tall and stylishly dressed. Instead of the quick pace she walks more slowly now; a hip replacement makes her cautious. She has good health and a sense of humor. We talk every Sunday, and she is cheerful, never complains, and always has an encouraging word for me. I am blessed!

Mothers are special and unique. One does not have to depreciate the role of fathers to recognize that uniqueness. Many must rely on memories of their mothers. No longer is she present; the voice is stilled, the smile a distant memory. Thank God for memory! Mothers are a gift from God.

Each child has his or her own memories; they are secret and special places and may cause a smile or tear or sometimes a cringe when remembering the insensitivity and thoughtlessness of children. A part of being a mother, I believe, is an innate quality of understanding and forgiving. There are exceptions. Not all memories are good ones, but these should not obscure the fact that remembering mothers is a good experience for the vast majority of people.

While all women are not biological mothers, all persons have mothers. I am especially mindful of those mothers who never bore children but who took unto themselves to be mothers to those born to another. Their pain, sacrifice, love, and nurturing were no less real because they did not carry the life within their bodies. In some inexplicable way they were one with that life they chose to claim. They loved that son or daughter in such deep and lasting ways that the meaning of mother was expanded beyond mere biological dimensions to a new spiritual and relational reality.

Mothers come in all sizes and colors. They speak different languages; they live in the city and in the country. Some have great learning from a university, some from the university of life, some from both. There are mothers of the rich and powerful, and mothers of the poor and powerless. All of them are special and precious.

Some know at once the special quality of a mother, while others learn of it over a long period of time. Many recognize her as a unique human being when they are no longer able to express appreciation to her. Possibly all of us sense that our expressions of appreciation and love for our mothers never quite match what we feel in our hearts. But I have a belief that mothers understand.

I now know why God said, "Honor your father and your mother" (Exodus 20:12 NRSV). And I do. I honor them as I do every day. Without them many of us would not be all that we are and hope to become.

Thank you, mothers everywhere, for loving us, your children, even when we were unlovable. Thank you, God, for this good and precious gift—Mother.

Hi, Dad! You are precious!

I am an avid sports fan. Like millions, I participate most frequently through the observance of athletic contests via television. With the seasons I move from one sports activity to the next—basketball and hockey, baseball and football. During football season I go to great lengths to try to arrange my schedule in order to watch my favorite football teams.

In a scene often repeated in football contests, the ball carrier receives the ball and with good blocking, skillful movement, and lightning speed dashes by opposing players to score a touchdown. Cheers come from the fans and congratulations from teammates. Nearly out of breath he goes to the sidelines and sits on the bench. The television cameras focus a close-up shot of the hard-breathing hero. He looks directly into the camera, aware that he is the center of attention of millions of television watchers, and raises his hand.

"Hi Mom!" he says. Almost never does he say, "Hi Dad!" or make an effort to be inclusive by saying, "Hi Mom and Dad!"

Rarely are songs or poems written about fathers. Frequently portrayed as not too bright or the butt of jokes, they have also a more negative characterization: stern, sometimes tyrannical, a figure to be feared or hated.

Unfortunately fathers are absent in many communities. No

image of them exists at all; there are no negative or positive models—just a void. Scripturally defined roles of fathers give them a prominent place in the family with almost absolute authority and major responsibility for determining the nature and character of family life. The role and prominence have altered with time. Fathers are now often perceived as an appendage to the family. But of course they are much more than that, unsung heroes for the most part.

They continue to receive few accolades for their loyalty and devotion. As a group they work harder and longer and live shorter lives. They are characterized more by those who fail to fulfill responsibly their fatherly roles than by the vast majority who do.

Each father is unique. Some are outgoing and interactive with family members. Others are reserved, more quiet and reflective. Some are unmistakably affectionate and expressive; others are subtle and find it difficult to express what is so close to their hearts. One must learn to look for the special secret sign of their love and affection, but it is there.

Some fathers take time with their children and are patient, teaching them frequently the lessons learned from their own fathers. I marvel at those who must chart their own course of fatherhood without having known their own father or determined the model they knew was inadequate or inappropriate.

Changing times test fathers everywhere. No longer are they in many instances the breadwinner of the family. Nor is it unquestionably conceded that father knows best. Yet the role of father is as important as ever, perhaps even more so, in these complex and changing times. Weaken the role of the father and you shake a basic foundation of the family. Responsible and responsive fathers are integral to stable family life and a healthy society.

Fathers. They are as different as the stars and just as precious.

Letter to Martin Luther King, Jr.

Dear Martin,
I write now as I have over the past several years on the anniversary of your birth. It is always a special time for me to

reflect on your life and work and your dream for America. It is a time to pause and to gain perspective.

The most jarring reality as I write is the awareness that more than two decades have passed since your tragic death. It does not seem possible. So much has happened and so much has not happened during these fleeting years. I expect, like me, you would look with considerable pride at the strides in racial inclusiveness made in the South these last years. But you would be saddened by what you would find throughout the North.

I must keep my promise made many years ago when I began writing to you on this occasion: to capture those bright spots in our seemingly never-ending struggle against bigotry and racism, and our efforts to create a genuinely racially inclusive society.

Some months ago I met Will Campbell. You remember him—that remarkable Southern Baptist preacher who played such a pivotal role in the early days of the Civil Rights movement. I have long admired him; I devour his writings and remember him with great respect and a sense of gratitude. He gave of himself at considerable cost at a time when the proponents of segregation and racism made white opponents pay a heavy price for their rebuke of personal and systemic bigotry. His book *Forty Acres and a Goat* details the pain, agony, and victories of the Civil Rights movement.

As I met Brother Will (as he likes to be called) I must admit that I, who had never been given to hero or celebrity worship, was in awe. He looked to me like a modern Amos: hair mussed, what is left of it, collar open, well-worn trousers and sport jacket. I suspect he walks with a cane more for effect than need.

As I chatted with him briefly, I thought: He is one of a long line of splendor, white men and women who refuse to acquiesce to a racist system and fought it when it was not only unpopular but physically risky for them and their families. We have not given them their due. Before we, especially black Americans, could appropriately acknowledge their courage and sacrifice, a social phenomenon emerged which created a wedge between us, black and white at least, that has not yet been fully dissolved.

On this occasion, Martin, as I remember your challenge—nay pleading—that we allow no one to pull us down so low as to cause us to hate, I remember these unsung heroes. Yours was a gospel of racial togetherness—unity, even when such a stance became as unpopular among many blacks as it was among whites.

As I remember you, I will recall the white Americans, South and North, who also had a dream. Among them are the countless men and women who created and sustained the underground railroad and enabled thousands of our forbearers to escape the tyranny of slavery. I remember and salute those abolitionists who by the power of words and deeds would not let the nation forget the potential of its greatness and the inherent rightness of its creeds and promises, although narrowly perceived. And, Martin, without brave and courageous politicians who risked careers and social standing, laws would not have been made or enforced that would ensure protection, rights, and equality under that law.

I remember these and so many more who stood up and many who paid the ultimate price, life itself.

There is my roommate, a native son of Mississippi, who understood and understands the wrongness of racism. Disavowed and rejected by family, turned away by his annual conference, he is disfigured as the result of an unsuccessful attempt on his life.

Another colleague, in Chicago, unrelenting in his opposition to racism, now combats it in its global dimension.

My friend in Kansas continues to make herself unpopular because of her persistence in attacking racism.

Then, Martin, there are my two brothers in South Carolina, one a pastor, the other a layman, who won't let those around them become satisfied with victories gained. They continue to point to the ever-present evidence of racism and bigotry in the Church and community.

A former college president, now living in the beautiful mountains of North Carolina, gave so much to this struggle, but he has never been appropriately recognized for his courage and caring. I remember and know that I am in part what I am because of who he is.

I remember with profound gratitude those ministers—Methodists and others—who had to leave their beloved Southland because the church they too loved did not understand or accept their gospel of racial inclusiveness and reconciliation.

Yes, Martin, thousands of men and women—ministers and teachers, editors and journalists, secretaries and clerks, farmers and factory workers, rich and poor from all walks of life—stood up against racism and all its manifestations. Without them the gains we celebrate today would not have been possible.

Martin, I know you would agree. What more appropriate time than your birthday to say to these brothers and sisters everywhere: Thank you for sharing the dream!

Sing the Resurrection song as never before!

Oh, if only I could step into a pulpit on Easter Sunday morning! How frustrating for a preacher not to be able to preach on the holiest of all days in the life of the Christian church. What an occasion it is—trumpets will sound, voices will be raised in song, hearts will be stirred, and the Good News proclaimed. He lives! He lives!

How I would prepare for the moment, molding and shaping the message with care given to each word, and looking for illustrations to highlight the drama of the Resurrection story. No worshiper ought to leave the church without being spiritually filled, indeed exhausted, yet crying for more. How I would do my best! What an opportunity to move from the routine to the extraordinary, and to be reminded of this audacious God who got the world's attention and has still not lost it in the face of formidable distractions.

Yes, Easter morning is the time to pull out all the stops. Even average preachers become eloquent on Easter. Let the message take over and the messenger will be surprised. Insights will be sharpened, hours spent laboring over the message will be rewarded, and souls touched in fresh new ways.

If I could lead a congregation in worship, I would stand just a little taller on Easter Sunday and sing with a little more gusto. My smile would broaden and my voice would laugh. There would be no mistake that this morning would be different from all the rest.

I would encourage the congregation to sing like the saints of old from their hearts, and to recall the ways in which the One who is the center of the singing has touched their lives in moments of joy or despair, faith or doubt, brokenness or reconciliation. Remembering Jesus in those private and personal ways, I would ask the congregation to sing as they have never sung before.

Then I would remind the worshipers about hope and ask them to remember all the people and places where hopelessness abounds, where citizens are abused by governments and governments dominated by other governments, and where men, women, and children are randomly shot and beaten. I would ask the congregation to remember those not far from the place where they sing who long ago lost any belief that life could make sense or be just. Yes, I would ask the congregation to look deep into the world's soul and see all the hopelessness in its awful rawness, and then sing about One who is the hope of the world!

I would greet each worshiper with a little more love, clutch each hand with a bit more tenderness, touch each soul with a great deal more care. What a privilege to be able to sing, to preach, and to give witness to the risen Lord.

But that's what ought to happen every Sunday in worship; for the Christian every Lord's day is Easter! Hallelujah!

Dwelling Places of Fear and Guilt

Fear is an awful place in which to dwell. If you remain in the room of fear it can suffocate you. But it is not a room that should be avoided; perhaps in reality it cannot. If you move in and out of the room of fear but do not dwell there, perhaps fear can even be redemptive.

I have known fear

I have known fear. The universal emotion of fear includes various degrees of intensity. I imagine I have experienced them all. But the ultimate fear is expressed in the phrase "scared to death!"

Fear has been described as "an emotion characterized by dread or expectation of harm; or the desire to escape or avoid harm, or the displeasure of something conceived as a power; especially reverence for supreme power; as, the fear of God."

Most of us live in the normal range of fear. We learn early to fear those places or circumstances that might cause us harm. There seems to be an innate fear of falling although it may simply be one of life's earliest lessons along with other traditional childhood fears. In time we grow out of them or put them in proper perspective so as not to fear unduly.

Deep psychological fears sometimes remain with us throughout life. Others become so stressful and debilitating as to require professional help in overcoming or coping with them.

Many of us have those unique fears that attach themselves to our psyche and won't let go. They're not overwhelming but are annoying. I have a fear of cats. It seems that whenever I enter a room, no matter how many others are present, the resident cat seeks me out, jumps into my lap, rubs against my leg, or simply lies across my feet. I have learned to hide this fear most of the time. These little unexplained fears make life more challenging.

Sometimes we all experience unavoidable fears of human living: making a mistake, looking foolish, being embarrassed, or failing! Often I dread making a decision for fear of its consequences or that it will be unpopular or misunderstood.

Some people become gripped by fear, unable to act. Life becomes a burden because the consequences seem so devastating. To do nothing appears the better alternative. The ways in which this kind of fear is manifested vary in their impact. It may cause one to avoid new experiences, new people and circumstances, thus closing life.

Russell Criddle in *Love Is Not Blind* observed, "People, most of them, hurt people they are afraid of."

Perhaps this is at the core of violence that results from religious and racial bigotry. Those who perpetrate such acts often commit them with an outward display of bravery and arrogance, sometimes drape themselves in militaristic symbols. Maybe they are not tough, strong, or brave after all, but are just fearful of those who become the objects of their wrath. In essence they are the objects of their fear.

The fear of death at some time touches us all. Many are preoccupied with it, others are interrupted by it. An unexplained lump, pain, or other physical symptom reminds us of our mortality, and so we contemplate death in fear.

Fear is an awful place in which to dwell. If you remain in the room of fear it can suffocate you. But it is not a room that should be avoided; perhaps in reality it cannot. If you move in and out of the room of fear but do not dwell there, perhaps fear can even be redemptive. Or, perhaps like me, you might even be scared to life!

Lent is for us

It is a familiar courtroom litany: "How do you plead?" "Not guilty!"

The common use of plea bargaining almost makes the guilty plea obsolete no matter how strong the evidence. One will plead guilty to a lesser charge and avoid the possibility of a conviction on a more serious offense. Perjury, the act of lying under oath, is not at all uncommon. The phenomenon of denying one's guilt, however, is not limited to a court of law.

Lent is a time to own one's guilt. It is counter-culture to a growing societal ethos which seeks to obviate guilt by rationalizations, legal maneuvers, technicalities, or a relativist ethic. In the midst of such a guilt-denying morass comes this Christian season which is glaringly out of step.

The question put to the Christian community in the season of Lent by the Supreme Judge of all courts is the familiar one: "How do you plead?" The response is, "Guilty as charged!" A contemporary gospel tune begins, "I was guilty of all the charges. . . ."

Whatever else Lent means to the Church and the individual Christian, there is the inescapable reality that we all fall short of what we desire for ourselves and of what God expects of us.

Some people wallow in their guilt. They seem to gain a strange satisfaction in rehearsing it. Sometimes it appears to be more important than forgiveness. Too many become comfortable with their guilt. In a peculiar sense it becomes a shield or method of avoidance. Guilt once acknowledged ends the matter. Nothing more is required. In its extreme form there is a glory in guilt. This sometimes becomes the focus of one's theology, or preaching, or living.

At the other extreme is guilt avoidance. Here corporately and individually great effort is made to deny guilt. The actions themselves are not denied, rather it is the assessment or meaning of them that is denied. They change character as they take on new meaning. Thus the deed does not become a misdeed, which removes any need to assume guilt. History records many illustrations of nations refusing to assume corporate guilt. Each of us can find in our own lives personal examples of this.

But Lent encapsulates us all. At a time when there seems such a tide of accusatory rhetoric it is a humbling relief. Here none escapes. Feminists stand guilty along with chauvinists. Victims of racial and religious bigotry assume their share of guilt as well as bigots and racists. Clergy so accustomed to pointing out the sins and failures of others acknowledge their own. Evangelicals, liberals, conservatives, or however one is named, are indistinguishable in their guilt. Political and economic systems cannot avoid the verdict under close scrutiny. Neither can nations.

Lent is not the season, however, to be overwhelmed by our guilt, but to recognize, acknowledge, and own it. To be guilty is

to be justly charged or responsible for one's misdeeds. The key is
to be justifiably charged.

When asked the awesome question, "How do you plead?"
after our life record is reviewed, our acts of commission and
omission enumerated, who of us can answer anything but
"Guilty as charged!"

We need to remember when the season comes: Lent is for us!

God's character includes judgment

No aspect of God's character and action has more prominence
in my thinking and theology than grace. God's grace puzzles and
grips me: to be loved unreservedly and undeservedly is still
mind-boggling. It is an ultimate ethic.

Nothing in Christian thought demonstrates God's grace more
dramatically than the sending of Jesus as Savior for the whole
world. To accept and experience him are life-altering. It is no
wonder that John Newton cried out, "Amazing grace, how
sweet the sound."

While grace and God's unending love are clearly central
themes of Christianity, Old Testament thought had an
important place for God's wrath. Both Old and New Testaments
promise God's judgment eminent and eschatological. I wonder
how God's displeasure is evidenced.

My own imperfections are all too clear to me. Like the apostle
Paul, the good I should do is the very thing I fail to do, and I often
do the wrong I should not. Many times I must have disappointed
and displeased God.

God does not miss such actions, inactions, or thoughts
however cleverly I try to conceal them. If God reveals and
responds to what pleases, surely God responds to what
displeases. How does God express wrath, disappointment, and
displeasure?

The taking of life today seems to come so easily and
effortlessly—even over a parking place—at a price far less than
thirty pieces of silver!

Surely God does more than weep over the city when God

observes how so many people are forced to live there in neglect, need, and deprivation. Is not God displeased over the failure of those who can make life more livable for others?

Does God simply turn away from the pain, ill will, and ill treatment of persons for a variety of reasons—color, gender, class, belief? What does God do when God is displeased? Is God capable of anger or wrath?

The fact that innocent and vulnerable children are abused, brutalized, and traumatized stirs in me emotions of rage and anger. So many are victimized personally and systemically. Is God moved less than I?

Is God oblivious to the nations where despots force their people to live in fear and want, where dissent is answered with death and torture?

A gracious God continues to give resources and riches to the human family. Ungrateful people ignore such a God, give nothing in return, and misuse these treasures. Values seem to be displaced and priorities confused. How long will God be mocked?

What does God do when God has had enough? How does God hold us accountable for our misdeeds? How does God judge a nation, a people, a tyrant, a bishop? I wonder!

On saving face

Saving face is a colloquialism that describes the effort to look as good as one can in the midst of a bad or unfavorable situation. Interestingly, the concept does not describe an effort to do good—only to look good! In the midst of difficult and sometimes compromising circumstances, one tries to emerge with some sense of pride and self-esteem. Often poor decisions and questionable conduct have been the result of an effort to save face.

Premarital sex among teenagers is more prevalent than most parents and adults want to acknowledge, approaching the norm rather than the exception. It is acceptable and expected behavior among many teenagers.

A teenaged couple, not intending to be in a compromising situation where they might engage in premarital sex, find themselves precisely in such a position. Each knows the sexual mores of peers. They reach that decisive moment when they can say "yes," "no," or "wait." Rushing through their minds are so many clashing values, but uppermost, "What will my friends think if I don't?" In order to save face a decision is made with consequences that are detrimental, yet seemingly not nearly as important as the appearance and place among peers.

Sometimes nations are tempted and forced to consider face-saving measures. A nation is the target of aggressive action by another, or by citizens of an unfriendly country. Some awful deed is done: a terrorist act, kidnapping, murder. The nation so transgressed against must be mindful of its image as a strong and powerful one, yet must save face in the international community. It contemplates what retaliatory action to take and perhaps responds with greater force than the act that was committed against it. Occasionally nations make unwise, important decisions in order to save face.

Pride is a powerful human characteristic. A sense of personal pride can result in noble or ignoble actions. One's self-esteem is important to one's self and to others. Respect by others is in part a measure of self-esteem. At times, however, acceptance and respect of others conflict with highest values or noblest actions. To look good among one's peers may require one to ignore a high value and right action.

Sometimes leaders and those who exercise great authority are met with this dilemma. A certain situation might challenge a decision or authority. Every parent has faced his or her authority being called into question by a child. To give in would make it appear that a son or daughter had actually won the dispute or forced the parent to capitulate. To save face a parent could exercise his or her authority even though it might not be in the best interest of the child, thus in a strange sense looking good but not doing good.

Christians, I suppose, are met daily with this dilemma. The Christian ethic calls for a standard of behavior and conduct that may be contrary to community standards and peer expectations. To save face may mean compromising basic and fundamental values.

Leaders inside and outside of the Church are met from time to time with difficult ethical decisions requiring the hard choice to save face by doing and saying what they believe to be required.

To paraphrase a familiar verse, For what would it profit a person to save face and lose self-respect?

Life's lumps can be unfair

Life is not always fair, and neither are people and circumstances. But sometimes you just have to take it!

My earliest discovery of this bit of wisdom came as I grew up in a community and era in which adults were always right. Their word was law. Children did whatever the teacher instructed. In the judgment of parents, there was no such thing as the child's point of view.

In our community it seemed all adults took responsibility for the neighborhood youth. They possessed community permission not only to scold or chastise a child other than their own, they could even spank when circumstances demanded it. Thus, someone was always watching us!

On one occasion a group of us boys got into some mischief. One of my chums said a bad word, as we termed it in those days. An adult overheard; his gaze immediately fell on me. He called me over, gave me a lecture, and said he would tell my mother. (My father was away in military service during those war years.)

True to his word, the neighbor told my mother I had used profanity. I told her, as I told him, that I did not use the words I was accused of saying, but the matter was closed with my mother. Mr. King said I did and that settled it. I got a spanking I did not deserve.

I never have forgotten the lesson I learned that day about life. Sometimes you simply have to take what life and circumstances give—not all the time, but sometimes.

A former president of the United States made news headlines

when commenting on a sensitive and rather controversial issue by stating, "Life is not always fair!" He was verbally attacked and criticized. But I, at eight years of age, knew life was not always fair.

Some approach this inevitable slice of life as God-ordained. Divine Providence foreordained certain events and circumstances that are unalterable. Try as one might or will, nothing can alter the inevitable.

I don't give such heavy theologizing to all such events. Frankly, I think God is too busy to be involved in all the situations we choose to attribute to God.

I am struck by how much mis-information and half-information shape our opinions and decisions. A popular American humorist once correctly observed, "The trouble with the world is that so many people know so much that ain't so!"

Sometimes impressions of others and by others are far from reality and truth. Yet they so color opinion that no amount of response or interpretation can or will change the situation.

I think all of us have at some time felt we were totally misunderstood or misjudged. Sometimes persons misinterpreted data; other times they had only partial data due to particular circumstances—to give more would violate confidences, or it was none of their business.

Such circumstances result in gossip, broken relationships, or unfair impressions. And you just have to take it.

Often what appears to be so is not. Events and circumstances all point to a logical conclusion. The appearance of truth is not always truth.

There was no way I could convince Mr. King I had not said those bad words. He knew my voice and was certain he had heard it. He was a highly respected man in our community. Thus my mother knew instantaneously that he would not report that I had said something I had not.

Circumstances, experiences, and judgments come in life that are sometimes undeserved, unfair, and inappropriate. They touch all of us. I had no idea that day that I would be given in addition to a spanking a valuable lesson in life.

Sin's companions

Of all the television evangelists, I liked him least. He seemed to have little place for grace in his preaching or theology. And he seemed somewhat self-righteous and mean-spirited. Yet the recent revelations of moral lapse and the discovery that he, too, has feet of clay bring no delight, only sadness.

I hurt for his wife, family, and congregation. I am certain that thousands who have been touched by his ministry, and his many television followers, are feeling a sense of devastation as the events come under public scrutiny. It is a sad day.

We seem to be a sex-obsessed culture. There are those obsessed with watching it and others obsessed with those who want to watch it!

Sexual immorality is characterized as sinful behavior in our Judeo-Christian tradition and in most religious traditions. United Methodism in recent years has sensed the need to be more definitive in a society that it considers has become too promiscuous.

The *Book of Discipline* of The United Methodist Church maintains:

> Although men and women are sexual beings whether or not they are married, sex between a man and woman is only to be clearly affirmed in the bond of marriage. Sex may become exploitive within as well as outside marriage. We reject all sexual expressions which damage or destroy the humanity God has given us as birthright, and we affirm only that sexual expression which enhances that same humanity, in the midst of diverse opinion as to what constitutes that enhancement [Paragraph 7.1(F)].

In more recent years our church has specifically stated that those who are to be set apart as moral and spiritual leaders, the ordained ministers, "are required to maintain higher standards represented by the practice of fidelity in marriage and celibacy in singleness" (Paragraph 402.2).

The highest standard of sexual behavior is expected of those calling themselves Christian. However, the standard involves faithfulness, relationship, and integrity and is not just about anatomical parts.

Sex is a good gift of God not to be abused or misused. What I sometimes fear we have done, however, is to elevate sexual transgression in a hierarchy of sin that places it in supreme prominence. It becomes the make or break transgression, the ultimate moral failure. Indeed, it almost holds the status of the unforgivable sin.

We dare not minimize the seriousness of sexual transgression, but neither should we trivialize nor minimize the many other ways we displease God and act in an immoral fashion. The words of Urban T. Holmes III in his *Spirituality for Ministry* remind us that "American religion is obsessed with the 'warm sins' such as sex," and fails to take proper cognizance of the "cold sins." These cold sins are no less demonic.

Racism, for example. Is there anyone who doubts the stain of racial separation and bigotry on the church of Jesus Christ, or what it has done to fracture our nation, or its immoral character and nature? Does one think God is less pleased with the racial bigot than the sexual transgressor?

Idolatry is another of these cold sins. We idolize the thing or person to which we give our ultimate loyalty. God comes second or third so often to family, spouse, business, fraternal allegiance, nation, race, or culture. Too frequently, even for those of us ordained and "set apart," career, place, mobility, and status take precedence in our lives and God stands in the wings.

I wonder what the Prince of Peace thinks of the ingenious ways we have created to destroy one another in the name of peace. What does God think of the manner in which even the faithful destroy persons by rumor and gossip, relegate others to inferior status, or totally ignore the needy and destitute? The sins could go on to illustrate the ways we disappoint and displease God.

It is too easy to be judgmental about the sins or moral lapses of others, or to create a hierarchal order of sin which leaves ours off the list altogether. God is not mocked or dissuaded by our clever manipulation. I fear each of us has sufficient sin to be saddened when a brother or sister falters. I do!

Lent reminds us that sin is a burden we need not bear

Even in her sleep she can get no rest. The guilt of her misdeeds pushes deep into her subconscious by day, rising to consciousness by night. The soul won't forget what the mind tries to put aside: greed, deception, murder. Lady Macbeth walks trance-like, attempting to wash her hands that she sees covered with blood. There is no water, no cleansing solution, yet she washes and cries, "Out, damned spot! Out, I say!—One: two: why then, 'tis time to do't—Hell is murky!"

We are more like Lady Macbeth than we dare to acknowledge or admit even to our private selves. The misdeed—a better word is sin—rarely approaches the taking of another life but is real enough to weigh us down. Sometimes its power interrupts sleep or makes waking hours unbearable.

Sin, democratic and inclusive, is by thought, word, or deed—often by all three. It is sometimes flagrant and obvious, unmistakable in its manifestation, or it can be subtle, disguised, seductive.

In a small volume that I use frequently for personal devotion entitled *A Book of Private Prayer*, Dom Hubert Van Zeller writes about a rare disease of the brain called agnosia, which renders the patient incapable of recognizing familiar objects. Father Van Zeller says, "But a sort of spiritual agnosia must be very common. We see sin, whether in ourselves or in other people, and do not recognize it." The problem is not in its unfamiliarity but rather that "its essential meaning has been forgotten. Even when we have it explained to us, we can forget it: We can go on not recognizing it for what it is."

At times sin is so endemic that it presents itself as law, tradition, custom or simply the way we do things. Because the community sanctions it, the wrong is redefined as right. But however many times voted so by the majority, wrong is never right. It is still sin.

On the other hand, sin is often characterized not by its nature but by its perpetrator. Thus it becomes confusing to the onlooker since its meaning changes from season to season, place to place, door to door.

Most of us live, however, with the soul confirming what the mind knows as transgression. No amount of pretense can trick that moral self. Not even title or position can change the meaning of the thought, word, or deed. It is inescapable. It finds us even in our sleep.

It is not necessary to define or list what I mean by sin. I might miss yours and you would feel safe, even self-righteous. Worse yet, you would see it in others and not yourself. Suffice it to say, it is that dimension of self that touches every human spirit.

The informed spirit knows sin only too well. The immature self simply succumbs or wallows in it. Sometimes we are overwhelmed by it; some ignore it. The stubborn fight it within and without. There is one who spoke for many when he implored, "What can wash away my sins?"

Lent is a time when the whole Christian community is reminded of a part of its inescapable nature. Here we are one: orthodox and reformed, conservative and liberal, first church and last church! It is a strange commonality, but our sin renders us all equal.

During Lent as we individually and corporately examine our sin, we recall the answer. We know the futility of self-cleansing purification rites. We know that we need not, like Lady Macbeth, be saddled forever with overwhelming guilt even in the face of our wrongdoing.

What can wash away our sin? The Christian hears the response, "Nothing but the blood of Jesus." In that blood is everlasting cleansing, centered in the cross of Christ, and in that Christ is found God's amazing grace.

Whether we win or we lose . . .

No one likes to lose! It matters not if the loss is an athletic contest or some other game. The loss of a girlfriend or boyfriend to another can cause grief. The loss of a loved one to death is devastating. And the loss of things—property, money, investments—can overwhelm.

But no one can go through life without losing. Championship teams lose. The good lose, the bad lose, and even the careful lose. There is an inevitability about loss. Life is not always a successful reality.

According to popular theology, winning or success comes to those who trust, have faith, are good, and who merely believe. Of course this is not a new way of interpreting life and events, but it is more widespread and increasingly characterizes the culture of many societies.

When success and winning are linked to deity it becomes a matter of less than passing interest. Calamity has long been held to be the result of either unfaithfulness or the displeasure of God. Inversely, good fortune and success are the results or rewards of faithfulness and a pleased God.

The view is too simplistic. Moreover it makes God fickle and encourages manipulative adherence. Such views cause untold grief and guilt among many of the faithful who experience loss, calamity, or inexplicable suffering. It is a "Jovian" dilemma.

This strange mixture of a secular philosophy and strongly held theology, even if not always fully thought through, results in this success/blessings milieu. Succeed at all costs! Win at all costs! Get the blessing at all costs!

Some build their life or career on such thinking; they choose a church or religion on the basis that it will provide such assurances. Then it happens—they lose. They fail or disaster strikes. Soon such persons discover they have the theology for winning and succeeding but none of losing and failing. Devastated, they are pushed to the edge of despair, sometimes worse.

How easy to believe in a God when life is full of evidence that such a God exists. The harvest is plentiful, family comfortable, career secure, and love unshakable.

But what does one do when the crops fail, the investments are lost, or the infant is born with a deformity? What does one do when he or she is not popular, promoted, or appreciated, misunderstood, maligned, or persecuted? What happens when one doesn't get the contract or bonus? Is the goodness or existence of God dependent on these things? I hope not, for, in the words of a popular book, indeed your god is too small and your faith is little more than a positive prescription for the good (successful) life.

We dare not trivialize the pain of losing; it is enormous. But neither stake your claim nor your ultimate meaning in it either. If we win or lose, we are the Lord's. If we are the Lord's, we have not lost.

When nothing goes right

On certain days I wish it were possible to avoid life, not the living of it, but the interacting with it. Then I would like to be an observer of only life's beauty, not its pains and awful contradictions, and be divorced from the sordid, from the conflict, and from some of life's harsh realities.

Years ago there was a New York (or at least a Bronx) phrase, "I shoulda stood in bed!" In proper Illinoisese it translates, "I should have stayed in bed."

The phrase is the admission of the human spirit that nothing is going right. Routine tasks become disasters. Life seems to fall apart before your eyes. Even your problems have problems! Yes, it would have been better simply to remain in bed and not greet the day.

But we can't stay in bed. However much we want to refrain from interacting, life is unavoidable. We must make decisions, take stands, engage in issues, and relate to persons. How does the responsible self not interact with vital justice issues?

Then we have the more personal challenges: kids, spouse, colleagues, parishioners, or pastor. In spite of one's best efforts conflicts remain; an overwhelming standoff is reality. Reconciliation, even clarity, seems impossible.

Leadership has its own peculiar vicissitudes: difficult and complex decisions where often no good choice exists, only the best among poor choices; the lonely place where and when no one can join you.

What does it mean to be a mature self, a faithful Christian, a responsible leader? It means in part that when you want desperately to stay in bed, you get up! On those days when your rational self convinces you to seek to avoid life, you must meet it instead. Life is not to be observed; it is to be lived. Ultimately, I think, all decisions by Christians are stewardship decisions. Each of us must finally answer, "What did you do with what God gave you?" We were not placed in the world simply to function as human sponges, merely absorbing and not giving to life in return. To be a responsible self is to engage life, interact with it, struggle with it, contribute to it, somehow make it better than you found it.

A kind of psychology and theology that distorts life is characterized by a line from a popular tune that suggests that life is beautiful when "everything's going my way!" When life doesn't go our way we can become hard to live with, or in our deepest response, despair and frustration set in. Perhaps that's what finally happens to the victims of suicide. They meet that place in life when it doesn't go their way, and they are unable to cope.

What the Christian life is about is coping, but more than that it's engaging life and finding fulfillment in it even when everything's not going our way. It is not nearly as important that everything go my way as it is that everything go God's way. From what I know about me, I suspect may be true of you as well: my way is not always God's way.

What does it mean to be Christian in the last decade of the twentieth century? It means what it has always meant: to embrace life, confront it, challenge it, and shape it; to try to discern what God would have you do and be and then do it. And trust God to do the rest.

Harvests of Hope

The future is not closed. It is open and thus allows for new possibilities. Today's adversities need not be tomorrow's catastrophes. Hope is realistic because it provides both human and divine participation. The linking of God's power and human effort gives confidence in the future, and where human effort is insufficient, the promise of God never to leave us alone provides the balance. However sordid, blemished, or difficult, life can be beautiful.

Hope has its beginnings in the promises of God

● Pastors, neighbors, and some members of the congregation helplessly watched flames soar through the roof. One can only imagine what went through the minds of parishioners who had stored a lifetime of memories and experiences in that local church.

Several days later the pastor led me through the charred sanctuary, destroyed but sufficiently saved to make restoration possible. In the face of such devastation, the pastor talked about the future with hope. She and the congregation had been tested, but, undergirded by their faith, they proved sufficient.

● The effects of chemotherapy are hardly noticeable. He rarely complains about the painful ordeal he experiences weekly. He makes a Herculean effort to maintain his routine schedule and tries to assure me and others he's doing fine. I watch him and am humbled by his bravery, sense of faith, and hope. I wonder if I could be so brave under similar circumstances.

● When the teenager discovered her pregnancy, she panicked. Thoughts of running away, then of suicide, bombarded her. What could she do? It would cause her parents pain and embarrassment; her dreams of college and career now would go unfulfilled. Life was over, she said: "I really blew it!"

Now, some years later, she is picking up the pieces of her life, sustained by loving parents and a caring community. It is still tough but she assures me, "I'm going to make it!" Her hope in the future sustains her. Her faith has been strengthened, and she has discovered a compassion in the church she did not know existed and an inner strength which surprises her.

Although much of life is comprised of pain and misfortune,

sometimes the weight of suffering permanently mars the beauty of life for many. Others who experience the beauty of life in all its fullness have their joy shattered by some devastating misfortune—an indiscretion, a disease, an illness, an accident, or death. Their world, once filled with joy and happiness, seemed to crumble overnight.

Hope, faith, and determination are words that can become mere cliches, especially when spoken by those not experiencing the difficulty. Yet they reflect realities without which life could be a giant game of chance with predetermined winners and losers. Hope allows us to see beyond the now to the not yet. Jürgen Moltmann, in his book *The Theology of Hope,* has said, "Hope alone is to be called realistic, because it does not take things as they happen to stand or to lie, but as progressing, moving, things with possibilities of change."

The future is not closed. It is open and thus allows for new possibilities. Today's adversities need not be tomorrow's catastrophes. Hope is realistic because it provides both human and divine participation. The linking of God's power and human effort gives confidence in the future, and where human effort is insufficient, the promise of God never to leave us alone provides the balance. However sordid, blemished, or difficult, life can be beautiful.

How does the Christian sing?

If lucky, they sleep six or more in a room in an unsightly transient hotel. Other fortunate ones spend the night on cots in a church fellowship hall or gymnasium.

Those not so fortunate wrap themselves in cardboard boxes and sleep on heated grates, trying to keep warm against the winter night's chill. They are the thousands of homeless men, women, children, and families.

It is inconceivable and unconscionable that a nation as enlightened and as rich as ours should have so many citizens who have no place to live. It is a national scandal!

There are those for whom our elaborate and often ineffective welfare system is not responsive. They eat haphazardly, even out of garbage cans, or not at all in this wealthy nation. Ironically these scenes often occur only blocks from our national capitol.

The growing number of persons now counted among the third generation of families where the heads of households have never been gainfully employed is staggering. Statistics revealing the decline of the unemployment rate conceal the number of the permanently unemployed. They do not know and some will never know the meaning and dignity of work; they will not experience the satisfaction of contributing.

The new poor include factory workers, farm-related business people, and farm families who have lost everything—land, home, income, self-respect, and now hope!

The almost epidemic number suffering from AIDS—babies, teenagers, mothers, fathers, young adults, men and women, homosexual and heterosexual—is frightening to contemplate and even more catastrophic when the future is projected.

War and terrorism appear to be everywhere. No continent escapes war's destruction, and the nuclear threat hovers constantly.

Never-ending racial tensions at home and abroad stand as constant reminders of the depth of hatred and ill-will among us.

Other indications reflect the brokenness in the human family—increased drug use, child and wife abuse, family deterioration, and growing materialism.

In the face of such a litany of despair and hopelessness, how does the Christian sing Christmas carols and hallelujahs? Does our "Merry Christmas!" suggest an insensitivity to those who are more depressed by the season than elated? Are we merely oblivious and callous to the plight of these disinherited? Perhaps the Christian has become insulated from the hurts of brothers and sisters, or worse, has come to accept their place as a peripheral and marginalized segment of the human family.

Is the event of Christmas some cosmic contradiction to the reality of life itself? No!

The Christian understands the meaning of what God did for humankind that first Christmas morning. It is not a contradiction to life but an answer to it.

The Christmas message is found most uniquely and profoundly in the words of Paul:

> Who shall separate us from the love of Christ? Shall tribulation, or distress, or persecution, or famine, or nakedness, or peril, or sword? . . . No, in all these things we are more than conquerors through him who loved us. For I am sure that neither death, nor life, nor angels, nor principalities, nor things present, nor things to come, nor powers, nor height, nor depth, nor anything else in all creation, will be able to separate us from the love of God in Christ Jesus our Lord. (Romans 8:35, 37-39)

This is the reason we sing hallelujah!

On planting for a faithful harvest

It's harvest time. Farmers are going into the field to assess their crop yield for the season. The yield for most will be disappointing if not disastrous due to circumstances beyond their control. They planned well, tilled the soil conscientiously, rose early and worked late, but the harvest will not be commensurate with their efforts.

Life at times treats everyone that way. I think of pastors and congregations who give of themselves unselfishly. They are faithful in preparation, conscientious in attending to pastoral responsibilities, evangelistic in outreach, caring in social response, but the results of these efforts are meager. Membership and attendance continue to decline, soon followed by frustration, guilt, and discouragement. We are accustomed to being rewarded for our good works.

Without a relationship between actions and consequences, life would be chaotic and totally unpredictable. There must be a sensible rhythm that assures consequences from certain actions: some will result in disaster, others in joy, sadness, or pain. Diligent study will result in learning. Proper care of crops will bring in a good harvest.

But circumstances and conditions outside of one's control may defy this general principle of life. Love sometimes begets rejection, loyalty is met with unfaithfulness, and caring responded to with abuse.

If you train children in the way they should go, when they are older they may depart from it! In many instances, too, achievements of children are met not with compliment and encouragement but with criticism and more pressure. Neither does it automatically follow that great evangelistic and socially relevant preaching will result in full sanctuaries and ever increasing membership.

At times the normal rhythm of life seems off balance. The predictable is unpredictable, and the unexpected seems unfair. It comes to every life and to all persons: farmers and teachers, bishops and pastors, business people and laborers, rich and poor, young and old. Our best efforts are met with less than rewarding results, disaster, and failure. A corner of life marked *Out of your control!* lets you know that ultimately you cannot determine the consequences. You can love, but you cannot assure that you will be loved in return. You can plant but cannot promise growth, preach but not guarantee conversion.

When one gives his or her best to those things that make for success and it is not achieved, it makes the doing of right seem futile. Some throw up their hands and shout, "What's the use?" If one's faith and theology have no place for failure despite one's own actions, if goodness must always be rewarded with goodness and proper and attentive farming with abundant crops, the lack of success is even more challenging.

What we can control is our own sense of stewardship and faithfulness in doing a job well, being faithful to God, life, and relationships, and planting seeds for crops or seeds of love. This is what we can do.

And when it is our turn to experience the lack of reward for our efforts, rejection of our love, or the inadequate yields at harvest time, we might remember and give thanks to God for those times when the harvest was plentiful and beyond what we gave of time, love, attention, and faithfulness. Praise God for the abundance that came not because of us, but often in spite of us.

So plant again, continue to love, preach and witness untiringly, forgive and embrace—for in the doing of them is faithfulness. Faithfulness has its own reward and its own harvest that the world cannot give or take away.

Explorations of Selfhood

We do all we can to form right opinion, make correct judgments, and to be consistent with the highest religious and ethical values we know. Yet somewhere along life's road, mistake will find us. We hope that it will not be life-threatening or otherwise harmful. It can be one of life's valuable lessons learned in the faith journey.

Missions accomplished

I have watched with considerable admiration and awe those who set for themselves seemingly impossible and dangerous goals.

A paraplegic plans a cross country solo trip in a wheelchair, pushing the wheels until his or her hands are blistered. A group plans a mountain climbing expedition, selecting one of the most difficult mountains in the country. A young woman with a dog team plans a freezing and hazardous journey across Alaska.

Such heroic efforts are undertaken daily for the sheer satisfaction of completing an important, difficult task. Those who will never attract media attention or celebrity status undertake more common challenges every bit as brave and rewarding.

On one occasion I was invited to participate in a meaningful ordination service in a neighboring state. When one of the ordinands approached the kneeler I noted that she was blind. As she knelt in the silence of that sacred moment, one could hear faint and muffled cries. Then our hands went on her head and the bishop's voice cracked as he pronounced the words of ordination, making her a full elder in the ministry of The United Methodist Church.

I can't even begin to imagine all the peaks and valleys this servant of God experienced to achieve this goal. It must have been hard, difficult, and sometimes discouraging, but she persevered.

Those who walk across a stage in commencement exercises— high school, college, or graduate school—often find the walk short, the handing of the diploma or degree quick. But the journey was long for those who were the first in their families to accomplish this goal. They likely have achieved this moment against a mountain of odds. No member in the family was able to assist with homework assignments, even those first ones as a child.

These youth felt no peer pressure to study, excel, or to go on to higher education. Certain students found little support from an educational system that had already given up on them. They had no money for college or university, only the prayers and best wishes of their families.

These are truly unsung heroes. Perhaps no academic awards or recognition will be given them, but those who know they are heroes will beam and weep.

A relatively recent phenomenon is the second career person, who in mid-life changes from a successful career to another. The church has been blessed with those who have come into full-time ministry or Christian service from other professions.

These persons and their families have often literally given up everything—a handsome salary, or sometimes two, their home, and their life's savings to pursue education or service in the church. Some will study in a field that seems foreign to them; studying, writing papers, and taking exams will be a challenge.

But the moment comes when, after all the sacrifice, they earn the degree, receive ordination, and a church appointment.

So many accomplish so much that is not always acknowledged or appreciated. But it does not go completely unnoticed. A few friends will be proud. Family members understand. Those who have achieved have an exhilarating sense of accomplishment. And God smiles!

The test of truth

Truth has been lauded as a supreme virtue, but telling the truth is not always easy despite instructions of parents and teachers from our early years. We heard the story of how little George Washington, even in the face of parental reprimand, told the truth. How many times have children been reminded of this model as the standard of behavior?

The biblical injunction is equally clear, "The truth shall make you free." And "honesty is the best policy" has been the slogan of many business enterprises.

In spite of well-intentioned admonitions, I have found that truth-telling is not always easy. We sometimes shade the truth, tampering with it a bit. We also use the half truth, which is a mixture of total untruth with truth. We all know about the little white lie, a kind of suspension of the ethical. It suggests that on occasion the community sanctions the deliberate casting of words that are contrary to reality.

Perhaps some people always and under every circumstance tell the truth. They live under the courtroom directive to "tell the whole truth, nothing but the truth. . . ." It is a noble goal and commendable effort.

Most persons have discovered the ambiguity of truth-telling. Lying is an unpardonable offense, we are told, until we learn about the exceptions: when someone comes to the door who is not welcomed, or when old enough but not tall enough to pay full admission to the movies or adult fare on the bus or train.

Are there times when truth-telling is essential and times when it is not? A spouse asks about a new hair style, dress, or suit, and then with great anticipation awaits your response to the question, "How do I look?" A friend wants your honest opinion about his or her actions or attitude and says, "Tell me the truth, I can take it!"

What does it mean to tell the truth in love? Usually it means we share the truth about others rather than the truth we are willing to hear about ourselves. I am of the opinion that most of us couldn't bear all the truth that could be told about us.

Perhaps there is truth, and then there is truth: the truth spoken by political candidates when they share their vision, their intentions to implement programs if elected; the truth expounded from the pulpit about life and morals, decisions and choices; truth in words spoken to a sweetheart or spouse upon which relationships are built.

What is truth when talking to a person with low self-esteem who is needing affirmation and support, encouragement and grace? Or when it is clear, in spite of all the best intentions and the greatest desire, that the ministry is not the place where a person should seek to give his or her life commitment?

"The whole truth and nothing but the truth, so help you God" is a necessary courtroom expectation, but what would it mean to repeat those words before uttering opinion, counsel, advice, or consolation?

I have faced ethical dilemmas most of my life. They are dilemmas precisely because two equally valuable propositions have been presented. Total truth in one instance meant a person might be harmed, or not telling the truth meant a life literally might be saved. I have also faced an awesome and frightening moment when the truth would place my own life in jeopardy, and it was crystal clear to me what I had to do and say: tell the truth, the whole truth, and nothing but the truth!

At a time when deception seems so commonplace, and when we have little confidence that the mere placing of a hand on a Bible and swearing what one says will be the whole truth, it's no perfunctory exercise to give pause to the meaning of truth. To tell the truth is still a desired and expected virtue that holds together and gives meaning to relationships, covenants, and social intercourse. But living up to the virtue is no simple act.

Past mistakes become lessons in wisdom

We all make mistakes. To do so is to err in judgment, opinion, or deed. Some are minor and of little significance. Others can be catastrophic with life-changing consequences. To live without making mistakes is impossible. Eventually they will find us.

Mistakes of judgment may come after several options have been considered and weighed and then the most desirable one is selected. One learns at some future time that it was not the best decision.

Sometimes when our trust of others is violated, either by strangers or by those we think we know well, we learn that to have trusted so unreservedly was a mistake. Some mistakes have no resulting ill effects. Preoccupied, a driver goes through a stop sign when no other traffic is nearby to be at risk in this violation of traffic safety. Another preoccupied driver enters the highway from the wrong side, driving against the traffic, and meets an approaching vehicle head on. The mistake is costly and can be deadly.

Some mistakes are made with clear intent and are called mistakes only afterward. Life presents various options and circumstances. Sometimes these violate one's personal values or societal or group principles or ethics. For a variety of reasons, known most clearly to the violator, a person chooses to disregard those values or principles. Faced with guilt or the consequences of the deed, one says with utter sincerity, "I made a mistake!"

Who has not wished that words uttered could be retrieved or rephrased? At the time they seemed so appropriate and conveyed the truth that sought expression. But the words did not result in the intended good, or the harm desired was far too harsh in a more reflective moment. Before anyone could tell you, you knew that a terrible mistake had been made. The test of life is to minimize errors of judgment, opinion, or deed and to monitor one's thoughts, words, and actions in such a way that mistakes of great proportion or impact will not occur. It begins with heeding an early parental admonition: think before you speak! It continues as we learn to weigh actions and consequences. Life teaches us to be steady and careful. We learn something of the interdependence of the human family. Individuals do not live in isolation. Whether in a family, office, assembly line, or on the farm, actions and opinions affect more than a single individual. Thus, mistakes can impact others in a significant manner.

I doubt if the phrase "honest mistake" can be found in a dictionary, but the term comes from the book of life. It recognizes the collective wisdom of people that at times a good that was intended resulted in an opposite consequence. Life understands the impossibility of the human spirit or mind in every instance to accomplish the good desired by right judgment, opinion, or deed. So Life is gracious and withholds a severe judgment in acknowledgment of an honest mistake. I have known this grace.

We do all we can to form right opinions, to make correct judgments, and to be consistent with the highest religious and ethical values we know. Yet somewhere along life's road, Mistake will find us. We hope that it will not be life-threatening or otherwise harmful. It can be one of life's valuable lessons learned in the faith journey.

Hugh White, an early American statesman, once said, "When you make a mistake, don't look back at it long. Take the reason of the thing in your mind, and then look forward. Mistakes are lessons of wisdom. The past cannot be changed. The future is yet in your power."

Owning up to one's deeds

Being held accountable for one's misdeeds is tricky! Most don't like it, and neither do those who have to hold others accountable. It is a thing I like least about being a bishop.

I remember hearing my grandmother say as she was about to "save" this grandson by not sparing the rod, "This hurts me more than it hurts you!" In no way could she make me believe those words in light of the existential reality I was about to experience. On other occasions during my younger years, I thought to myself in the face of some harsh parental decision, "If you loved me you wouldn't do this to me!"

I have learned that these two childhood dilemmas are no less real in adulthood. Reaping what one sows or being held accountable is one of life's hard and perplexing lessons. One experiences both internal and external accountability. With internal accountability, life seems to have its own court and judge, and metes out its verdict on misdeeds committed. Jesus' admonition on reaping and sowing best illustrates this form of liability that does not involve blame from other persons. Even deeds done in secret have a self-revelation that accuses the accused more severely than any external judgment. It is life's way of holding us responsible.

One's attitude and behavior impose inevitable results. Think and act a certain way, and consequences will follow as surely as night follows day. Something in life says no! or yes! Life is not always consistent, however. Often the wicked do prosper and the righteous suffer, and so life itself appears to be unfair and capricious.

Regarding external accountability, there are those chosen or given the authority and responsibility of holding others accountable. They may be parent, teacher, supervisor, bishop, or committee. This awesome, painful duty is often more difficult due to the knowledge of one's own glaring imperfections.

The task is yet more complex. I am impressed how frequently the child's attitude repeats itself when adults are confronted by the consequences of their own deeds. From the mouths of adults, expressed in attitudes sometimes subtle and sophisticated, is the same childlike response, "If you loved me, you wouldn't do this to me." The reasoning suggests that love obviates accountability. However, sometimes the most loving act is to say, "Stop! No! No more!"

Few parents escape feeling guilty when correcting or holding a child accountable for his or her actions. Every teacher, supervisor, or colleague knows the agony of having to make decisions that adversely affect the lives, even if momentarily, of those cared for and loved. I suppose that is what my grandmother meant when she said it hurt her to hurt me. Yet because of her love, and not her lack of it, she had to hold me accountable. It is indeed tricky!

We do not live in a morally neutral world. We cannot abuse or violate moral principles, body, mind, spirit, one another, or even environment without some day answering for our acts. We must answer to the external or to the internal. And surely we must answer to God.

I always hope that those who hold others accountable for their misdeeds will do so with fairness and compassion, justice and mercy. But whatever others may do, I am assured that "God was in Christ personally reconciling the world to himself—not counting their sins against them . . . so that in Christ we might be made good with the goodness of God" (II Corinthians 5:19-21 Phillips).

On being your best self among your critics

Sometimes there's just nothing you can do! The human personality is a complex phenomenon. Occasionally you will encounter one that is totally bewildering. Try as you may, your ability to understand its functioning leaves you puzzled and mystified. The problem is accentuated when one attempts to adjust or accommodate to such a puzzling reality. You will never be able to please some people. At least it seems that way. The situation becomes more problematic when, through special relationships such as living, working, worshiping, or even recreating together, you are unable to avoid the individual.

Your efforts will not satisfy their expectations. You will be either too fat or too thin, too tall or too short, too passive or too aggressive, too talkative or too quiet, too early or too late—too something or another!

The self-esteem of many people is largely predicated on what others think of them. They give greater or lesser importance to the value judgment depending on who the other is. While people generally want to be liked or accepted by others, it is crucial and sometimes necessary that there be acceptance by particular persons—family member, spouse, pastor, parishioner, colleague, or business associate.

The dilemma results when for some unknown reason acceptance does not materialize. The average person will seek to discover the problem and make some adjustment where that seems to be reasonable. He or she hopes to continue or establish a meaningful relationship.

Some make many accommodations, sometimes minor and frequently major, only to discover that these have made no appreciable difference. When the adjustment does not alter the behavior of the other, there is a sense of futility and frustration.

Then it happens: having failed to gain the acceptance desired, a person turns on self. He or she becomes depressed, forlorn, and begins to question his or her own worth. Self-esteem begins to diminish.

Or another equally unhealthy response occurs: hostility or anger appears. In both instances, however, the object of the response is self. Anger and hostility, especially if not expressed but only internalized, affect only the one who is angry and not the object of the anger. Persons walk around like human time bombs or with their nerves on edge, while the one who may have been the "cause" of the anger is unscathed. Indeed, that person may be oblivious to the other's emotional state or may delight in it.

Too many people are emotionally crippled because they let others determine the assessment of their worth and self-esteem. In its extreme this can be the consequence of prejudice, racism, and sexism. These cause their victims to attempt to accommodate themselves to the unrealistic and unachievable expectations of others.

The mature self recognizes the appropriate place and need for others' values, acceptance, and judgments, but refuses to be tyrannized by them.

No one can live isolated from other human beings. Interaction with other people is not only inevitable, but it makes for wholeness of life. There are those who can see aspects of our behavior and attitudes perhaps more objectively than we can ourselves. When they genuinely care, their assessment can be helpful to our self-understanding. However, when they are insensitive or even callous, their assessment can be more destructive than helpful and may not be accurate.

You will be able to tell. Listen, assess, and be open to hear criticism as well as compliments. Then you, and you alone, must make the final assessment of self. Be honest with yourself, even tough, but never forget you are a valued human being of infinite worth created by a good and wise God. Don't be afraid to change when that is appropriate. However, don't hesitate to be your full, best self even in the face of criticism. The line is fine, but the mature self is able to discern the difference.

You will never be able to please everyone, so stop trying and do your best with what God has given you!

Jackie Robinson is more than a baseball hero

"Play ball!"

I always look forward to the arrival of America's favorite pastime. When baseball season arrives, the landscape and activity of America change.

"Take me out to the ball game" will be played and sung as crowds join in jubilantly. Hot dogs with mustard, peanuts, and Cracker Jack will be consumed by the ton. That's a part of the game of baseball as experienced from coast to coast. It is as integral to our national life as voting and the Fourth of July. It is our history; we have shaped it and been shaped by it.

Shortly after World War II, the game of baseball, as well as the face of American life, was radically changed. I was in elementary school and I knew something exciting, important, and dramatic had taken place, but I was not fully aware of its import and impact. Neither was America.

There were shouts and cheers; men on street corners and in barber shops argued, debated, and speculated. Some stated their disbelief; others vented anger and said, "It's about time!" Even during worship services time was taken to acknowledge the historic event, and prayers of thanksgiving were offered.

On April 10, 1947, the Brooklyn Dodgers baseball management announced it had purchased a contract of one who would be known the world over as Jackie Robinson. The following day he began his major league career, and the game would never be the same. Neither would America!

Some have forgotten; others have never known. I recall a Sunday afternoon discussion with my youth group in 1962. James Meredith had become the "first Negro" to be admitted to the University of Mississippi. Riots had erupted, making it necessary to send out twelve thousand federal troops to ensure his safety and restore law and order. As the youth discussed this event, they were almost unanimous in their opinion that James Meredith should not enroll at Ole Miss. They reasoned, to my astonishment, that if white people did not want black people to attend *their* school, we should not impose ourselves where we were not wanted.

I desired to push the point and said, "What would baseball be like today if Jackie Robinson had taken that position?"

With blank stares on their faces, they responded, "Who's Jackie Robinson?"

I was sad. For the first time in my life, I felt old! I knew the meaning of the generation gap before it became vogue.

How could Jackie Robinson have been forgotten so quickly? Although he was appropriately acknowledged by election to baseball's Hall of Fame in 1962, he represented more than a baseball hero to millions. He demonstrated character. He took the abuse and taunts of baseball fans and players alike. To this day I cannot forget that one of today's most popular television and radio baseball announcers was unrelenting in his attacks on Jackie.

Jackie Robinson taught in his own way the importance of competence and skills, and he demonstrated that barriers thought to be insurmountable were indeed conquerable. In fact, he permitted America to live out its old yet unrealized creeds. What he did was to show America what it could be in all facets of its life, including its religious life. For many began to say, "If baseball and Jackie Robinson can do it, so can we!"

There is no doubt in my mind that the single event in April, 1947, changed the course of American history. A brave man named Branch Rickey and a braver man named John Roosevelt

Robinson brought the nation one step closer to the realization of its yet unachieved noble principles.

Robert K. Greenleaf has written in his *Servant Leadership,* "We are sorely in need of strong ethical leaders to go out ahead to show the way, so that the moral standards and the perceptions of the many will be raised, and so that they will serve better with what they have and what they know!"

We in the church can still learn a lesson from Mr. Rickey and Mr. Robinson.

Keys to home for the "prodigal" and "perfect"

The words of the old spiritual seem to strike an almost universal cord: "Sometimes I feel like a motherless child a long way from home." Who has not at some time felt such loneliness, emptiness, utter despondency? It's more poignant when such aloneness is the result of one's own impulsiveness.

Except for the nativity narrative, probably no New Testament story is more popular than the one we call the parable of the prodigal son (Luke 15:11-32). It has all the elements of high drama: hero, villain, defeat, success, vindication, even a bit of titillation.

Some read the story as a justification of the inevitability of the riotous life or the sowing of one's wild oats. On the other extreme is the self-righteous condemnation of the prodigal.

The words of Caleb Colton, a nineteen-century English cleric, are instructive: "Let us not be too prodigal when we are young, nor too parsimonious when we are old. Otherwise we shall fall into the common error of those who, when they had the power to enjoy, had not the prudence to acquire; and when they had the prudence to acquire, had no longer the power to enjoy."

Perhaps the story's timeless appeal lies in the ability of the reader's identification with one or more, or perhaps all, of its central characters. Few have avoided feeling at some time like the prodigal—the lost one. Life at home seemed too constraining, the rules too strict, the old place too boring and suffocating. Besides, the community was too conservative, unimaginative, and unredeemably parochial.

After taking as much as one could endure, departure was inevitable. Sometimes the scene was amiable; parents gave reluctant blessing to the departure, which made it less difficult but still necessary. Unfortunately on other occasions, the scene held harsh and angry words, tears, the slamming of a door, and screeching tires. For the one who has gone, the reality of life, harsh and unfriendly, sometimes comes too quickly. In spite of oneself there is a longing for home with all its routine, boredom, and parochialism, but also its heretofore unappreciated security and love.

Some have known this sense of prodigality only second hand; others know it all too well and remember when the soul sang, "Sometimes I feel like a motherless child a long way from home."

Then there are the dutiful ones, those who always seemed to please the folks. They always made good grades, were popular, obedient, reliable, ideal—yet taken for granted. Their perfection never needed or received special time or attention. Always there when parents called, they caused no trouble and were home by curfew. Yet oddly, they never felt fully appreciated. Their virtues seemed overlooked.

How many parents have escaped that awful feeling of watching helplessly as a child made what was clearly a poor or unwise decision? In spite of one's best efforts, the son or daughter moved to a far off country and the parents knew how painful would be the consequences. Sometimes they simply said, "Well I guess you'll have to learn the hard way!" Or they wept late at night and prayed constantly for their prodigal.

An exhaustive published work of the life of a noted clergyman, entitled *Harry Emerson Fosdick: Preacher Pastor Prophet* by Robert Moats Miller, contains a memorable line as recalled by young Fosdick. As he prepares to leave for college his father says, "My boy, you keep the key and you let it be a symbol to you as long as you live that you can come home any time, from anywhere, and come in without knocking."

Perhaps this finally is the appeal of the ancient New Testament story—disgrace, love, the forgiving character of the parent who won't abandon the child even when the child abandons the parent. The parent welcomes the lost one, celebrates the return, and simply lets the prodigal keep the key with the assurance that home will always be there. Isn't that what God through the gift of Jesus Christ says to all of us—faithful or prodigal?